TEACHER'S PET PUBLICATIONS

LITPLAN TEACHER PACK
for
The Alchemist
based on the book by
Paulo Coelho

Written by
Susan R. Woodward

© 2008 Teacher's Pet Publications
All Rights Reserved

Copyright Teacher's Pet Publications 2008

Only the student materials in this unit plan (such as worksheets, study questions, and tests) may be reproduced multiple times for use in the purchaser's classroom.

For any additional copyright questions, contact Teacher's Pet Publications.

www.tpet.com

TABLE OF CONTENTS - *The Alchemist*

Introduction	7
Unit Objectives	9
Reading Assignment Sheet	10
Unit Outline	11
Study Questions (Short Answer)	15
Quiz/Study Questions (Multiple Choice)	25
Pre-reading Vocabulary Worksheets	45
Lesson One (Introductory Lesson)	65
Non-fiction Assignment Sheet	87
Oral Reading Evaluation Form	80
Writing Assignment 1	82
Writing Assignment 2	91
Writing Assignment 3	108
Writing Evaluation Form	84
Vocabulary Review Activities	96
Extra Writing Assignments/Discussion ?s	100
Unit Review Activities	111
Unit Tests	117
Unit Resource Materials	179
Vocabulary Resource Materials	199

ABOUT THE AUTHOR

Paulo Coelho

Paulo Coelho was born August 24, 1947 in Rio de Janeiro, Brazil to Pedro Queima Coelho de Souza and his wife, Lygia. Coelho's parents did not share in their son's dream of becoming a writer, and even went so far as to have him twice institutionalized in a mental hospital for attempting to pursue his dream. The treatment in the hospital did nothing to make Coelho conform to his parents' wishes; in fact, he became rebellious. He got involved with the hippie movement in the 1960's as it spread through Brazil, embracing progressive politics and joining the peace and love generation. His creative explorations led him to the theatre, to journalism where he published an alternative magazine called *2001*, and to the Brazilian rock scene where he wrote lyrics for famous Brazilian singers such as Raul Seixas, Elis Regina, and Rita Lee.

His involvement in the hippie movement led Coelho to explore various types of mysticism and spirituality. He was highly influenced by the works of Aleister Crowley, and even joined an organization known as the Alternative society, which defended the individual's right to free expression. After being detained, questioned and tortured by a group of paramilitaries, Coelho decided to tame his radical behaviors. A chance meeting with a stranger in Amsterdam led Coelho to turn his life toward Catholicism and to walk the medieval pilgrim's route, the road to the Cathedral of Santiago de Compostela. This route across northern Spain is known as St. James's Way. This experience was recreated in his book *The Pilgrimage: Diary of Magus* (1987).

In 1988, Coelho wrote *The Alchemist*, based on *Tale of Two Dreamers* by Jorge Luis Borges, which was originally based on a tale from *The Thousand and One Arabian Nights*. Coelho's novel did not receive much critical acclaim, however, and the first edition only sold about nine hundred copies. When the publishing company decided not to reprint, Coelho refused to give up on the work, and signed with another publishing company. *The Alchemist* has since sold more copies than any other novel in Brazilian literary history.

Paulo Coelho and his wife, Christina, live in Rio do Janeiro where he serves as a member of the Board of the Shimon Peres Institute for Peace, a special counselor for the United Nations Educational, Scientific and Cultural Organization (UNESCO) for "Intercultural Dialogues and Spiritual Convergences," a board member of the Schwab Foundation for Social Entrepreneurship, and a member of the Brazilian Academy of Letters.

Major Works
Hell Archives (1982)
Practical Manuel of Vampirism (1986)
The Pilgrimage (1987)
The Alchemist (1988)
Brida (1990)
The Gift (1991)
The Valkyries (1992)
Maktub (1994)
By the River Piedra I Sat Down and Wept (1994)
The Fifth Mountain (1996)
The Manual of the Warrior of Light (1997)
Veronika Decides to Die (1998)
The Devil and Miss Prym (2000)
Fathers, Sons and Grandsons (2001)
Eleven Minutes (2003)

The Genie and the Roses (2004)
The Zahir (2005)
Like the Flowing River (2006)
The Witch of Portabello (2007)

INTRODUCTION *The Alchemist*

This LitPlan has been designed to develop students' reading, writing, thinking, and language skills through exercises and activities related to *The Alchemist*. It includes nineteen lessons, supported by extra resource materials.

The **introductory lesson** invites students, through Langston Hughes's poem "A Dream Deferred," to contemplate what happens when dreams are put off. Students will also discuss the tale of Narcissus from Greek mythology in preparation for understanding the novel's Prologue. Following the introductory activity, students are given a transition to explain how the activity relates to the book they are about to read. Following the transition, students are given the materials they will be using during the unit. At the end of the lesson, students begin the pre-reading work for the first reading assignment.

The **reading assignments** are approximately thirty pages each; some are a little shorter while others are a little longer. Students have approximately 15 minutes of pre-reading work to do prior to each reading assignment. This pre-reading work involves reviewing the study questions for the assignment and doing some vocabulary work for selected vocabulary words they will encounter in their reading.

The **study guide questions** are fact-based questions; students can find the answers to these questions right in the text. These questions come in two formats: short answer or multiple choice. The best use of these materials is probably to use the short answer version of the questions as study guides for students (since answers will be more complete), and to use the multiple choice version for occasional quizzes.

The **vocabulary work** is intended to enrich students' vocabularies as well as to aid in the students' understanding of the book. Prior to each reading assignment, students will complete a two-part worksheet for selected vocabulary words in the upcoming reading assignment. Part I focuses on students' use of general knowledge and contextual clues by giving the sentence in which the word appears in the text. Students are then to write down what they think the words mean based on the words' usage. Part II nails down the definitions of the words by giving students dictionary definitions of the words and having students match the words to the correct definitions based on the words' contextual usage. Students should then have an understanding of the words when they meet them in the text.

After each reading assignment, students will go back and formulate answers for the study guide questions. Discussion of these questions serves as a **review** of the most important events and ideas presented in the reading assignments.

After students complete reading the work, there is a **vocabulary review** lesson which pulls together all of the fragmented vocabulary lists for the reading assignments and gives students a review of all of the words they have studied.

Following the vocabulary review, a lesson is devoted to the **extra discussion questions/writing assignments**. These questions focus on interpretation, critical analysis, and personal response, employing a variety of thinking skills and adding to the students' understanding of the novel.

There are three **writing assignments** in this unit, each with the purpose of informing, persuading, or having students express personal opinions. Students will read a companion piece related to the Philosopher's Stone and the Elixir of Life and research alchemical concepts. They will give a presentation on their companion pieces and relate to *The Alchemist*. Students will create character journals. Students will select a quotation and write a persuasive essay about how the quotation relates to ideas presented in *The Alchemist*.

There is a non-fiction **reading assignment**. Students must read non-fiction articles, books, etc. to gather information about various forms of divination (tarot, i-ching, runes, etc.).

The **review lesson** pulls together all of the aspects of the unit. The teacher is given four or five choices of activities or games to use which all serve the same basic function of reviewing all of the information presented in the unit.

The **unit test** comes in two formats: multiple choice or short answer. As a convenience, two different tests for each format have been included. There is also an advanced short answer unit test for advanced students.

There are additional **support materials** included with this unit. The **Unit Resource Materials** section includes suggestions for an in-class library, crossword and word search puzzles related to the novel, and extra worksheets. There is a list of **bulletin board ideas** which gives the teacher suggestions for bulletin boards to go along with this unit. In addition, there is a list of **extra class activities** the teacher could choose from to enhance the unit or as a substitution for an exercise the teacher might feel is inappropriate for his/her class. **Answer keys** are located directly after the **reproducible student materials** throughout the unit. The **Vocabulary Resource Materials** section includes similar worksheets and games to reinforce the vocabulary words.

The **level** of this unit can be varied depending upon the criteria on which the individual assignments are graded, the teacher's expectations of his/her students in class discussions, and the formats chosen for the study guides, quizzes and test. If teachers have other ideas/activities they wish to use, they can usually easily be inserted prior to the review lesson.

The student materials may be reproduced for use in the teacher's classroom without infringement of copyrights. No other portion of this unit may be reproduced without the written consent of Teacher's Pet Publications, Inc.

UNIT OBJECTIVES *The Alchemist*

1. Through reading Paulo Coelho's *The Alchemist*, students will work both independently and in cooperative groups.

2. Students will demonstrate their understanding of the text on four levels: factual, interpretive, critical, and personal.

3. Students will explore the themes of following one's dreams, individuality, and love.

4. Students will be given the opportunity to practice reading aloud and silently to improve their skills in each area.

5. Students will answer questions to demonstrate their knowledge and understanding of the main events and characters in *The Alchemist* as they relate to the author's theme development.

6. Students will enrich their vocabularies and improve their understanding of the novel through the vocabulary lessons prepared for use in conjunction with the novel.

7. The writing assignments in this unit are geared to several purposes:
   a. To check the students' reading comprehension
   b. To make students think about the ideas presented by the novel
   c. To encourage logical thinking
   d. To provide an opportunity to practice good grammar and improve students' use of the English language
   e. To have students demonstrate their abilities to inform, to persuade, or to express their own personal ideas

   Note: Students will demonstrate the ability to write effectively to <u>inform</u> by developing and organizing facts to convey information. Students will demonstrate the ability to write effectively to <u>persuade</u> by selecting and organizing relevant information, establishing an argumentative purpose, and by designing an appropriate strategy for an identified audience. Students will demonstrate the ability to write effectively to <u>express personal ideas</u> by selecting a form and its appropriate elements.

8. Students will read aloud, report, and participate in large and small group discussions to improve their public speaking and personal interaction skills.

READING ASSIGNMENTS *The Alchemist*

Date Assigned	Assignment	Completion Date
	Assignment 1 Prologue & Part One through "And he vanished around the corner of the plaza."	
	Assignment 2 "The boy began again to read his book" to the end of Part One	
	Assignment 3 Beginning of Part Two to "I don't even know what alchemy is," the boy was saying, when the warehouse boss called them to come inside."	
	Assignment 4 "I'm the leader of the caravan" through "The boy thought of Fatima. And he decided he would go to see the chiefs of the tribes."	
	Assignment 5 "The boy approached the guard" through "'We'll leave tomorrow before sunrise,' was the alchemist's response."	
	Assignment 6 "The boy spent a sleepless night" through "I already know how to turn myself into the wind."	
	Assignment 7 "On the second day, the boy climbed to the top of a cliff" through "They mounted their horses."	
	Assignment 8 "I want to tell you a story about dreams" through the Epilogue	

UNIT OUTLINE *The Alchemist*

1	2	3	4	5
Intro: Dreams "A Dream Deferred" Narcissus myth PVR RA#1	Study ?s RA#1 Philosopher's Stone PVR RA#2	Study ?s RA#2 Quiz RA#1&2 Writing Assignment #1 PVR RA#3	Study ?s RA#3 Library/Media Center Non-Fiction Work: Divination PVR RA#4	Study ?s RA#4 Quiz RA#3&4 Characterization Posters PVR RA#5
6	7	8	9	10
Study ?s RA#5 Share Non-Fiction Assignments PVR RA#6	Study ?s RA#6 Quiz RA#5&6 Writing Assignment #2: PVR RA#7	Study ?s RA#7 PVR RA#8 Oral Reading	Study ?s RA#8 Quiz RA#7&8 Biblical Allusions	Vocabulary Work
11	12	13	14	15
Art Appreciation: Creative Response Descriptive Language	In-Class Creative Writing: Journal Entries (polishing)	Peer Response: Journal Entries Share Aloud	Extra Discussion Questions	In-Class Writing: Writing Assignment #3 (Persuasive)
16	17	18	19	
Day 1: Present Book Talks	Day 2: Present Book Talks	Review Materials	Unit Test	

Key: P = Preview Study Questions V = Vocabulary Work R = Read

STUDY GUIDE QUESTIONS

STUDY GUIDE QUESTIONS *The Alchemist*

Assignment 1
Prologue & Part One through "And he vanished around the corner of the plaza."
1. Why does the lake weep for Narcissus?
2. What is the most recent topic of the shepherd boy's comments to his sheep?
3. How does the boy spend his time when the merchant tells him he cannot shear his sheep until the afternoon?
4. What does the shepherd claim are "the only things that concerned the sheep"?
5. What had the shepherd's family hoped the boy would become as an adult?
6. What does the shepherd plan to do once he arrives in Tarifa before his anticipated meeting with the merchant's daughter?
7. Why does the shepherd decide to see the Gypsy woman?
8. Describe the shepherd boy's recurring dream.
9. According to the old man, what is the world's greatest lie?
10. According to the old man, what is the one great truth on this planet?

Assignment 2
"The boy began again to read his book" to the end of Part One
1. Why does the shepherd decide against telling the baker what the old man had said about him?
2. What does the boy see when he climbs the stone ramp that led to the top of the castle wall?
3. What is the "principle of favorability" that the old man speaks of?
4. What happens immediately after the old man tells the boy that he "will have to follow the omens" in order to find his treasure?
5. What are Urim and Thummim?
6. According to the "wisest of wise men," what is the secret of happiness?
7. What causes the shepherd boy to become distracted and, as a result, lose sight of the young man who is holding his money?
8. After helping the candy seller erect his stall in the plaza, to what realization did the shepherd boy come?
9. What does the boy do to earn food to eat?
10. After the owner of the crystal shop tells the boy how expensive it is to get to Egypt, what does the boy say he wants money for?

Assignment 3
Beginning of Part Two to "I don't even know what alchemy is," the boy was saying, when the warehouse boss called them to come inside."
1. Why does the boy stay on the job with the crystal merchant?
2. In order to attract more business after working there for one month, what does the boy suggest that the crystal merchant allow him to do?
3. What are the five obligations outlined by the Prophet in the Koran?

4. Why didn't the crystal merchant ever go on a pilgrimage to Mecca?
5. What reason does the merchant tell the boy about why he would not go to Mecca now?
6. After another two months of working for the merchant, what idea does the boy have to bring more customers into the crystal shop?
7. Why does the merchant claim to feel worse than he did before the boy arrived to work for him?
8. When the boy tells the merchant that he is going to be leaving to return to his country to buy sheep, he asks for the merchant's blessing. What does the merchant say about the boy's journey home?
9. Where does the boy decide to go once he leaves the merchant's home?
10. Who befriends the boy on the journey?

Assignment 4
"I'm the leader of the caravan" through "The boy thought of Fatima. And he decided he would go to see the chiefs of the tribes."
1. How large is the caravan the boy is traveling with?
2. How does the Englishman spend most of his time during the journey?
3. How did the camel driver who befriended the boy come to be in this line of work?
4. Who are the mysterious hooded men who sometimes appeared?
5. What news does the caravan leader learn that causes the members to become more cautious while traveling, especially at night?
6. What does the Englishman call "the principle that governs all things?"
7. What is the "Emerald Tablet"?
8. What is the liquid part of the Master Work called?
9. What is the solid part of the Master Work called?
10. Who is Fatima?

Assignment 5
"The boy approached the guard" through "'We'll leave tomorrow before sunrise,' was the alchemist's response."
1. What "omens from the desert" does the boy share with the chieftains of the oasis?
2. Who was the boy who saved Egypt through his interpretations of the Pharaoh's dreams?
3. What decision does the head chieftain make about the boy's visions?
4. What causes a loud, thundering sound and throws the boy to the ground?
5. According to the man on horseback, what is "the quality most essential to understanding the Language of the World?"
6. Who is the man on horseback?
7. What is the fate of the commander of the enemy battalion?
8. What words does the alchemist say that echo those of the old king?
9. When riding out into the desert, what does the alchemist instruct the boy to show him?

Assignment 6
"The boy spent a sleepless night" through "I already know how to turn myself into the wind."
1. Before leaving the oasis, where does the boy go?
2. What does the desert come to mean for Fatima?
3. How do the boy and the alchemist find food in the desert?
4. Why is the boy disappointed when the alchemist writes in the sand what is inscribed on the Emerald Tablet?
5. What is it that the alchemist tells the boy that he has to listen to?
6. According to the alchemist, what is worse than suffering?
7. What is one thing that, according to the alchemist, the boy still needs to know?
8. What do the armed tribesmen find in the alchemist's bag?
9. Why don't the tribesmen take what is in the alchemist's bag?
10. After they are captured by a tribe, what does the alchemist claim that the boy is able to do?

Assignment 7
"On the second day, the boy climbed to the top of a cliff" through "They mounted their horses."
1. What does the desert ask the boy to explain to it?
2. When the desert tells the boy that it cannot help him, who does it suggest that the boy call on for help?
3. When asked who taught the boy the language of the desert and wind, what is the boy's reply?
4. Who is the third "person" the boy is told to ask for help from?
5. What is the chief's plan for the two men who wanted to end the bet with the boy?
6. How does the sun claim to know about love?
7. According to the boy, why does alchemy exist?
8. Why does the wind "scream with delight?"
9. What legend did the Arabs recount for generations thereafter?
10. What feat does the alchemist perform at the monastery?

Assignment 8
"I want to tell you a story about dreams" through the Epilogue
1. Describe the dream the alchemist tells to the boy.
2. What did the centurion say that was remembered for all time?
3. What warning does the boy's heart whisper as he is about to climb a large dune?
4. What does the boy see when he finally reached the top of the dune?
5. As the boy wept at the sight that beheld him, what does he notice in the sand?
6. What does the boy do when he sees the omen?
7. Describe what happens when the refugees from the tribal wars approach the boy.
8. What piece of advice does the leader of the refugees give the boy before he leaves?
9. How does the boy finance his journey back to Spain?
10. What does the boy find beneath the sycamore tree in the ruined church?

STUDY GUIDE QUESTIONS ANSWER KEY *The Alchemist*

Assignment 1
Prologue & Part One through "And he vanished around the corner of the plaza."

1. Why does the lake weep for Narcissus?
   It weeps because each time Narcissus knelt beside the lake's banks, the lake's only beauty was reflected in Narcissus's eyes.

2. What is the most recent topic of the shepherd boy's comments to his sheep?
   The shepherd boy talks to the sheep about the daughter of a merchant that he'd met last time he traveled into the town.

3. How does the boy spend his time when the merchant tells him he cannot shear his sheep until the afternoon?
   He talks with the merchant's daughter and becomes so engrossed in talking with her that he found himself wishing the day would never end and that the merchant would keep him waiting for three days.

4. What does the shepherd claim are "the only things that concerned the sheep"?
   The only things that concerned the sheep were food and water.

5. What had the shepherd's family hoped the boy would become as an adult?
   The shepherd's family had wanted him to become a priest, so he went to seminary school.

6. What does the shepherd plan to do once he arrives in Tarifa before his anticipated meeting with the merchant's daughter?
   The shepherd plans to exchange his book for a thicker one, fill his wine bottle, shave, and have a haircut before meeting with the merchant's daughter.

7. Why does the shepherd decide to see the Gypsy woman?
   He wants the Gypsy woman to interpret a recurring dream.

8. Describe the shepherd boy's recurring dream.
   He has twice dreamt that a child came and played with his sheep. Suddenly, the child grabbed the hands of the shepherd and they were transported to the Egyptian Pyramids. The child told the shepherd that if he went there to the Pyramids, he would find a great treasure. However just as he was asking the child the location of the treasure, the shepherd woke up.

9. According to the old man, what is the world's greatest lie?
   He says that the world's greatest lie is that "at a certain point in our lives, we lose control of what's happening to us, and our lives become controlled by fate."

10. According to the old man, what is the one great truth on this planet?
    The one great truth is that "whoever you are, or whatever it is that you do, when you really want something, it's because that desire is originated in the soul of the universe. It's your mission on earth."

Assignment 2
"The boy began again to read his book" to the end of Part One

1. Why does the shepherd decide against telling the baker what the old man had said about him?
   He decides that it is better to leave things as they were and not to cause any anxiety for the baker. The old man had told the boy that the baker had once desired to travel, but he had opened his shop first in order to make the money. Now he will never travel.

2. What does the boy see when he climbs the stone ramp that led to the top of the castle wall?
   He is able to see the African coast as well as all over the city.
3. What is the "principle of favorability" that the old man speaks of?
   The old man says that it is the beginner's luck because "there is a force that wants you to realize your Personal Legend; it whets your appetite with a taste of success."
4. What happens immediately after the old man tells the boy that he "will have to follow the omens" in order to find his treasure?
   A butterfly flutters between the old man and the boy. The boy suddenly remembers that his grandfather once told him that butterflies are a good omen.
5. What are Urim and Thummim?
   They are two stones taken from the golden breastplate of the old man that can be used for divination. When asked an objective question, Urim is a black stone that signifies "yes" and Thummim is a white stone that signifies "no."
6. According to the "wisest of wise men," what is the secret of happiness?
   The wisest of the wise men says that the secret of happiness is "to see all the marvels of the world, and never to forget the drops of oil on the spoon."
7. What causes the shepherd boy to become distracted and, as a result, lose sight of the young man who is holding his money?
   The shepherd boy is distracted by a beautiful sword at the market. He takes his eyes off his "friend" who is holding his money, supposedly to buy camels to go to Egypt, and the "friend" disappears with the cash.
8. After helping the candy seller erect his stall in the plaza, to what realization did the shepherd boy come?
   He realizes that although the candy seller spoke Arabic and he spoke Spanish, the two had been able to understand one another perfectly. He concludes that there must be a language that does not depend on words.
9. What does the boy do to earn food to eat?
   The boy cleans the crystal seller's glasses in the store's front window. While he did so, two customers came in to buy crystal.
10. After the owner of the crystal shop tells the boy how expensive it is to get to Egypt, what does the boy say he wants money for?
    The boy says that he wants money to buy some sheep.

Assignment 3
Beginning of Part Two to "I don't even know what alchemy is," the boy was saying, when the warehouse boss called them to come inside."
1. Why does the boy stay on the job with the crystal merchant?
   The merchant treats the boy fairly and pays him a good commission for sales.
2. In order to attract more business after working there for one month, what does the boy suggest that the crystal merchant allow him to do?
   The boy wants to build a display case to place outside the store to attract more customers. In this way, the boy can sell more crystal and earn more money to buy sheep.
3. What are the five obligations outlined by the Prophet in the Koran?
   The five obligations are: To believe in the one true God, to pray five times a day, to fast during Ramadan, to be charitable to the poor, and to make a pilgrimage to the holy city of Mecca at least once in a lifetime.

4. Why didn't the crystal merchant ever go on a pilgrimage to Mecca?
   He intended to do it when he earned enough money. Once the business got going, he felt he couldn't leave the shop in someone else's hands long enough to go to Mecca.

5. What reason does the merchant tell the boy about why he would not go to Mecca now?
   The merchant says that it's the thought about someday going to Mecca that keeps him alive. If he were to realize his dream, then he believes that he will have no reason for living.

6. After another two months of working for the merchant, what idea does the boy have to bring more customers into the crystal shop?
   He has observed how many people complain that there is no place to get something to drink after making such a climb to the top of the hill. He asks the merchant to sell tea in crystal glasses so the customers might be enticed to buy the glassware once they've had tea in them and seen how beautiful they are.

7. Why does the merchant claim to feel worse than he did before the boy arrived to work for him?
   The boy has shown the merchant possibilities he's never dreamed of, but the man does not like change. The merchant now knows of things he should be able to accomplish, but he simply does not want to do them.

8. When the boy tells the merchant that he is going to be leaving to return to his country to buy sheep, he asks for the merchant's blessing. What does the merchant say about the boy's journey home?
   The merchant says that just as he knows that he will never go to Mecca, the boy will not be returning home to buy his sheep.

9. Where does the boy decide to go once he leaves the merchant's home?
   He decides to join a caravan heading towards Egypt and the Pyramids.

10. Who befriends the boy on the journey?
    An Englishman who is studying alchemy desires to find an alchemist who is reported to be living in the desert. The two hundred year old alchemist supposedly holds the secret to the Philosopher's Stone and the Elixir of Life.

Assignment 4
"I'm the leader of the caravan" through "The boy thought of Fatima. And he decided he would go to see the chiefs of the tribes."

1. How large is the caravan the boy is traveling with?
   There are nearly two hundred people and four hundred animals within the caravan crossing the desert.

2. How does the Englishman spend most of his time during the journey?
   He spends most of his time reading books.

3. How did the camel driver who befriended the boy come to be in this line of work?
   The man used to own an olive orchard, but when the Nile flooded the land and ruined his orchard, he was forced into another line of work.

4. Who are the mysterious hooded men who sometimes appeared?
   The hooded men are Bedouins who do surveillance along the caravan route. They report any news about thieves or barbarian tribes to warn the caravans.

5. What news does the caravan leader learn that causes the members to become more cautious while traveling, especially at night?
   He learns that there are tribal wars taking place in the desert, and the caravan begins to travel in silence and keep its fires lower so as not to draw attention to themselves.

6. What does the Englishman call "the principle that governs all things?"
   He says that the principle that governs all things is called the Soul of the World.
7. What is the "Emerald Tablet"?
   It is an emerald upon which the most important text in the literature of alchemy, containing only a few lines, had been inscribed.
8. What is the liquid part of the Master Work called?
   The liquid part of the Master Work is called the Elixir of Life. It has the power to cure all illnesses and to prevent aging.
9. What is the solid part of the Master Work called?
   The solid part of the Master Work is called the Philosopher's Stone. A small sliver of the stone has the ability to transform large quantities of any metal into gold.
10. Who is Fatima?
    Fatima is a young woman who lives at the oasis. At first glance when they meet at a well, the boy falls in love with her. At every opportunity, the boy tries to meet Fatima at the well so that he can talk to her.

Assignment 5
"The boy approached the guard" through "'We'll leave tomorrow before sunrise,' was the alchemist's response."
1. What "omens from the desert" does the boy share with the chieftains of the oasis?
   The boy has seen a vision of men with swords attacking the oasis, so he decides to warn the chieftains of a possible onslaught.
2. Who was the boy who saved Egypt through his interpretations of the Pharaoh's dreams?
   The boy's name was Joseph.
3. What decision does the head chieftain make about the boy's visions?
   The chieftain decides that he will heed the warnings and arm his people the next day, although it is against tradition to carry weapons in an oasis. For every ten enemies killed by the weapons, the boy will receive one piece of gold. If no enemies attack, in order to keep the weapons from refusing to work when needed in the future, one of the weapons will be used on the boy.
4. What causes a loud, thundering sound and throws the boy to the ground?
   A man dressed in black astride a white horse challenges the boy saying, "Who dares to read the meaning of the flight of the hawks?"
5. According to the man on horseback, what is "the quality most essential to understanding the Language of the World?"
   That quality is courage.
6. Who is the man on horseback?
   The man on horseback is the alchemist that has been sought by the Englishman.
7. What is the fate of the commander of the enemy battalion?
   Because he broke the Tradition of the oases, the commander is condemned to death without honor. He is hanged from a dead palm tree.
8. What words does the alchemist say that echo those of the old king?
   "When a person really desires something, all the universe conspires to help that person to realize his dream."
9. When riding out into the desert, what does the alchemist instruct the boy to show him?
   The alchemist tells the boy to show him "where there is life in the desert." The boy follows the intuitions of his horse that stops by some rocks in the desert. When the alchemist puts his hand in a hole near the rocks, he pulls out a cobra.

Assignment 6
"The boy spent a sleepless night" through "I already know how to turn myself into the wind."
1. Before leaving the oasis, where does the boy go?
   He goes to see Fatima to say good-bye, and to tell her that he will be back.
2. What does the desert come to mean for Fatima?
   The desert now represents the hope for the boy's return.
3. How do the boy and the alchemist find food in the desert?
   The alchemist sends his falcon out to hunt each day, and it brings back game for them to eat.
4. Why is the boy disappointed when the alchemist writes in the sand what is inscribed on the Emerald Tablet?
   It is written in a code he does not understand, so it makes no more sense to him than the Englishman's books.
5. What is it that the alchemist tells the boy that he has to listen to?
   The alchemist tells the boy to listen to his heart.
6. According to the alchemist, what is worse than suffering?
   The alchemist tells the boy that the fear of suffering is worse than the suffering itself.
7. What is one thing that, according to the alchemist, the boy still needs to know?
   The alchemist says that "before a dream is realized, the Soul of the World tests everything that was learned along the way."
8. What do the armed tribesmen find in the alchemist's bag?
   They find a small flask filled with liquid and a yellow glass egg that is slightly larger than a chicken egg.
9. Why don't the tribesmen take what is in the alchemist's bag?
   When the alchemist tells them that the liquid is the Elixir of Life and that the glass egg is the Philosopher's Stone, they merely laugh and do not believe him.
10. After they are captured by a tribe, what does the alchemist claim that the boy is able to do?
    The alchemist tells the tribal leader that the boy can transform himself into the wind.

Assignment 7
"On the second day, the boy climbed to the top of a cliff" through "They mounted their horses."
1. What does the desert ask the boy to explain to it?
   The desert wants to know what love is.
2. When the desert tells the boy that it cannot help him, who does it suggest that the boy call on for help?
   The desert tells the boy to call on the wind for help.
3. When asked who taught the boy the language of the desert and wind, what is the boy's reply?
   The boy states that his heart taught him the language.
4. Who is the third "person" the boy is told to ask for help from?
   The wind tells the boy to ask heaven (the sun) for help.
5. What is the chief's plan for the two men who wanted to end the bet with the boy?
   The chief plans to remove them from their positions because "true men of the desert are not afraid."

6. How does the sun claim to know about love?
   The sun tells the boy that it knows about love because it is aware that if it came even a little bit closer to the earth, everything would die, and the Soul of the World would no longer exist. Because the sun and the Soul of the World work together to cause the plants to grow and the sheep to survive, the sun gives the world warmth, and the Soul of the World gives the sun a reason to exist.

7. According to the boy, why does alchemy exist?
   Alchemy exists so that "everyone will search for his treasure, find it, and then want to be better than he was in his former life."

8. Why does the wind "scream with delight?"
   The wind is delighted that the sun does not know everything because it could not answer the boy's question about how to turn himself into the wind. The wind wants to "tell every corner of the world that the sun's wisdom had its limitations."

9. What legend did the Arabs recount for generations thereafter?
   They told the tale of the boy who had "turned himself into the wind, almost destroying a military camp, in defiance of the most powerful chief in the desert."

10. What feat does the alchemist perform at the monastery?
    The alchemist turns lead into gold. He breaks it into four pieces: one for the monk for his generosity, one for the boy to make up for what the alchemist had taken from him to give the general, one for himself, and one for the monk to hold for the boy if he were to ever need it.

Assignment 8
"I want to tell you a story about dreams" through the Epilogue

1. Describe the dream the alchemist tells to the boy.
   A man in Ancient Rome had two sons: a soldier and a poet. An angel told the man in a dream that one of his sons' words would be remembered throughout time. When the man died, he asked the angel to tell him what words his son the poet had written that were so profound. The angel replied that it was the soldier's words to a Jewish rabbi that were remembered.

2. What did the centurion say that was remembered for all time?
   "My Lord, I am not worthy that you should come under my roof. But only speak a word and my servant will be healed."

3. What warning does the boy's heart whisper as he is about to climb a large dune?
   "Be aware of the place where you are brought to tears. That's where I am and that is where your treasure is."

4. What does the boy see when he finally reached the top of the dune?
   He sees the great Pyramids of Egypt.

5. As the boy wept at the sight that beheld him, what does he notice in the sand?
   He notices that where his tears fell in the sand, a sacred scarab beetle came scuttling up. He believes it is an omen.

6. What does the boy do when he sees the omen?
   He begins to dig in the sand with his bare hands thinking that his treasure is buried there.

7. Describe what happens when the refugees from the tribal wars approach the boy.
   Refugees from the tribal wars accost him and rob him of the gold piece the alchemist had given him. Believing the boy is burying more gold, they make him dig in the sand to give it to them. When nothing is produced, they beat him savagely. They planned to kill the boy, but the leader tells them to leave him.

8. What piece of advice does the leader of the refugees give the boy before he leaves?
   He tells the boy not to believe in dreams because he once, on the very spot where they now stood, had a dream that he was in an old church in Spain, and he found gold beneath a sycamore tree growing in the ruins of the sacristy. He said that he was not so stupid as to cross the desert because of a dream.
9. How does the boy finance his journey back to Spain?
   He goes back to the monastery where the alchemist had turned the lead into gold. The alchemist had asked the monk to hold a piece of the gold for the boy if he should ever need it. The boy claims the gold and uses it to get back to the churchyard in Spain where he once spent the night with his sheep and where he had his dream about the Pyramids.
10. What does the boy find beneath the sycamore tree in the ruined church?
    He finds a conquistador's treasure that had been buried there. The boy gives 10% to the gypsy woman who had interpreted his dream, and he uses the rest to go back to Fatima.

MULTIPLE CHOICE STUDY/QUIZ QUESTIONS
The Alchemist

Assignment 1
Prologue & Part One through "And he vanished around the corner of the plaza."

1. Why does the lake weep for Narcissus?
    A. It had been able to see its own beauty in Narcissus's eyes; it wants him back.
    B. Narcissus left with a woman and it feels neglected.
    C. It is grieving the loss of Narcissus.
    D. Narcissus was brutally murdered.

2. What is the most recent topic of the shepherd boy's comments to his sheep?
    A. He tells the sheep how rich he will be after selling their fine wool.
    B. He tells the sheep that he will have to sell them to the shearer in town.
    C. He tells the sheep that they will travel together to foreign lands.
    D. He tells the sheep about the merchant's daughter he hopes to see in town.

3. How does the boy spend his time when the merchant told him that the shepherd could not shear his sheep until the afternoon?
    A. He talks with the merchant's daughter.
    B. He takes his sheep to another merchant.
    C. He reads his new book.
    D. He spends the time sleeping.

4. What does the shepherd claim are "the only things that concerned the sheep"?
    A. They care about getting to another pasture in a far away land.
    B. They are concerned that they will be slaughtered for meat.
    C. They are concerned with being sold to a new owner.
    D. They are only concerned with food and water.

5. What had the shepherd's family hoped the boy would become as an adult?
    A. They wanted him to become a healer.
    B. They wanted him to become a shepherd like his father.
    C. They wanted him to become a priest.
    D. They wanted him to become a merchant.

6. Which of the following is NOT something the shepherd planned to do once he arrived in Tarifa before his anticipated meeting with the merchant's daughter?
    A. He planned to take a rest after his long journey.
    B. He planned to fill his jug with wine.
    C. He planned to get a shave and a haircut.
    D. He planned to buy a new book.

7. Why does the shepherd decide to see the Gypsy woman?
    A. He wants her to interpret a recurring dream.
    B. He wants her to tell his fortune about the merchant's daughter.
    C. He wants her to tell him about his father.
    D. He wants her to make a love potion to give to the merchant's daughter.

8. Describe the shepherd boy's recurring dream.
    A. He dreamed about seven thin cows that ate seven fat cows yet grew no bigger.
    B. He dreamed of becoming a wealthy merchant, but it all turned to dust.
    C. He dreamed about his own death.
    D. He dreamed of being taken to the Pyramids and told of a treasure.

9. According to the old man, what is the world's greatest lie?
    A. The world's greatest lie is that people were meant to be happy.
    B. The world's greatest lie is that people's lives are controlled by fate.
    C. The world's greatest lie is that people have the free will to do as they wish.
    D. The world's greatest lie is that people cannot see into the past or the future.

10. According to the old man, what is the one great truth on this planet?
    A. All people can see both the past and the present if they are open to it.
    B. There is no such thing as free will.
    C. People have absolutely no control over their own destinies.
    D. Our deepest desires originated in the soul of the universe.

Assignment 2
"The boy began again to read his book" to the end of Part One

1. Why does the shepherd decide against telling the baker what the old man had said about him?
    A. He thinks the baker will not believe him.
    B. He does not care if the baker knows or not; it's not up to him to tell the baker.
    C. He does not want to cause the baker any anxiety.
    D. The boy is jealous of the baker's desire to marry the merchant's daughter.

2. What does the boy see when he climbs the stone ramp that led to the top of the castle wall?
    A. He sees the gypsy woman talking with the old king.
    B. He has another vision about the Pyramids of Egypt.
    C. He sees the African coast.
    D. He sees the merchant's daughter with the baker.

3. What is the "principle of favorability" that the old man speaks of?
    A. It is also known as "beginner's luck."
    B. It is also known as "the survival of the fittest."
    C. It is also known as "being in the right place at the right time."
    D. It is also known as "the will of God."

4. What happens immediately after the old man tells the boy that he "will have to follow the omens" in order to find his treasure?
    A. A butterfly flutters between them.
    B. An eagle flies overhead.
    C. A wolf howls in the distance.
    D. The old man disappears.

5. What are Urim and Thummim?
    A. They are two stones used in divination.
    B. They are the "lead sheep" in the boy's flock.
    C. They are two men who bought the boy's sheep.
    D. They are two young boys who will accompany the boy to Egypt.

6. According to the "wisest of wise men," what is the secret of happiness?
    A. The secret of happiness is to be happy for others' fortunes without bitterness.
    B. The secret is to see the world's marvels without forgetting the oil in the spoon.
    C. The secret of happiness is to be happy with what you already have.
    D. The secret of happiness is to "bloom where you are planted."

7. What causes the shepherd boy to become distracted and, as a result, lose sight of the young man who is holding his money?
    A. He thinks he hears someone calling his name.
    B. He thinks he sees the old king in the crowd.
    C. He sees a beautiful woman.
    D. He sees a beautiful sword for sale in a vendor's stall.

8. After helping the candy seller erect his stall in the plaza, to what realization does the shepherd boy come?
    A. They speak different languages, yet they are able to understand one another.
    B. The candy seller stole his money when he was working.
    C. The boy who stole his money is the candy seller's son.
    D. He realizes that he wants to become a seller in the African bazaar.

9. What does the boy do to earn food to eat?
    A. He cleans glassware.
    B. He serves tables at the tavern where he'd met the thief, hoping to run into him.
    C. He sells his sheep in order to buy food.
    D. He cleans stalls for the camel herder.

10. After the owner of the crystal shop tells the boy how expensive it is to get to Egypt, what does the boy say he wants money for?
    A. He wants to buy a camel to take him to Egypt.
    B. He wants to buy some sheep.
    C. He wants to set up his own stall at the bazaar.
    D. He wants to return home to his family.

Assignment 3
Beginning of Part Two to "I don't even know what alchemy is," the boy was saying, when the warehouse boss called them to come inside."

1. Why does the boy stay on the job with the crystal merchant?
    A. He wishes to save enough money to buy a camel to go to Egypt.
    B. He is treated fairly and makes a good commission selling crystal.
    C. The boy has nowhere to go.
    D. He is saving enough money to return home to his family.

2. In order to attract more business after working there for one month, what does the boy suggest that the crystal merchant allow him to do?
    A. He asks the merchant to allow him to open a stall in the bazaar.
    B. He asks the merchant to let him paint a large billboard on the main road.
    C. He asks the merchant to allow him to place an ad in the local papers.
    D. He asks the merchant to let him build a display case for outside the shop.

3. Which of the following is NOT a part of the five obligations outlined by the Prophet in the Koran?
    A. One should pray five times a day.
    B. One should believe in the one true God.
    C. One should fast during Ramadan.
    D. One should tithe ten percent of his income to the church.

4. Why didn't the crystal merchant ever go on a pilgrimage to Mecca?
    A. He wanted to go to Rome instead.
    B. He never had enough money.
    C. He didn't want to leave his family.
    D. He didn't want to leave his shop in the hands of others while he was gone.

5. What reason does the merchant tell the boy about why he would not go to Mecca now?
    A. He says the dream of Mecca is what sustains him; without it, his life has no purpose.
    B. He cannot find anyone to take care of his shop while he is gone.
    C. His father is dying and he must be with him.
    D. He still does not have enough money.

6. After another two months of working for the merchant, what idea does the boy have to bring more customers into the crystal shop?
   A. He wants to build a large display case for the crystal.
   B. He wants to have a sale on crystal.
   C. He wants to sell tea in crystal glasses.
   D. He wants to import foreign crystal.

7. Why does the merchant claim to feel worse than he did before the boy arrived to work for him?
   A. The merchant's daughter has fallen in love with the boy; he disapproves of it.
   B. The boy has helped improve business, but the merchant doesn't want the extra work.
   C. The boy has shown him how he could accomplish things, but he hates change.
   D. The boy is a better seller than the crystal merchant.

8. When the boy tells the merchant that he is going to be leaving to return to his country to buy sheep, he asks for the merchant's blessing. What does the merchant say about the boy's journey home?
   A. He tells the boy that his daughter may accompany him to Spain as his wife.
   B. He begs the boy not to go because his business is doing so well now.
   C. He tells the boy that just as he will never go to Mecca, the boy will not be buying sheep.
   D. He wishes the boy well in his life.

9. Where does the boy decide to go once he leaves the merchant's home?
   A. He wishes to find the boy who robbed him and thank him for forcing him to take better care of himself.
   B. He decides to go to Salem to find the old king.
   C. He goes on a ship to Spain.
   D. He joins a caravan heading towards Egypt.

10. Who befriends the boy on the journey?
    A. He is befriended by the ship's captain.
    B. He is befriended by a man on horseback who takes him to the seashore.
    C. He is befriended by an Englishman in search of an alchemist in the desert.
    D. He is befriended by the boy who had originally robbed him.

Assignment 4
"I'm the leader of the caravan" through "The boy thought of Fatima. And he decided he would go to see the chiefs of the tribes."

1. How large is the caravan the boy is traveling with?
    A. There are over 200 people and 400 hundred animals in the caravan.
    B. There are only three: the Englishman, the boy, and the camel master.
    C. He is not traveling with a caravan.
    D. There are fifty people heading on a pilgrimage to Mecca.

2. How does the Englishman spend most of his time during the journey?
    A. He spends his time observing their surroundings and learning about the desert.
    B. He spends his time in prayer.
    C. He spends his time reading books about alchemy.
    D. He spends his time conversing with the boy about the universe.

3. How did the camel driver who befriended the boy come to be in this line of work?
    A. He was taken as a slave as a child by a group of camel drivers; it's all he knows.
    B. He left his position in the seminary to be able to see the world as a camel driver.
    C. He lost his olive orchard to a flood, and he needed to care for his family.
    D. He is from a family of camel drivers.

4. Who are the mysterious hooded men who sometimes appear?
    A. They are renegade warriors of various desert tribes.
    B. They are enemy spies from warring tribes in the desert.
    C. They are Bedouins who bring news and warnings about what is going on in the desert.
    D. They are escaped prisoners from Egyptian prisons.

5. What news does the caravan leader learn that causes the members to become more cautious while traveling, especially at night?
    A. A group of prisoners escaped from an Egyptian prison and are in the desert.
    B. The desert tribes are at war.
    C. There have been rumors of renegade thieves skulking in the desert.
    D. There are rumors that the Englishman is a wanted criminal and bounty hunters are looking for him.

6. What does the Englishman call "the principle that governs all things?"
   A. The Word of God governs all things.
   B. The Principle of Favorability governs all things.
   C. The Soul of the World governs all things.
   D. The Language of the World governs all things.

7. What is the "Emerald Tablet"?
   A. It is a jewel upon which the most important text of alchemy is inscribed.
   B. It is a magical stone that turns lead into gold.
   C. It is a rare jewel in the crown of the Egyptian pharaoh.
   D. It is a jewel in the armor of the old King Salem.

8. What is the liquid part of the Master Work called?
   A. The Nectar of the Gods
   B. The Cup of Truth
   C. The Elixir of Life
   D. The Fruit of the Vine

9. What is the solid part of the Master Work called?
   A. Ambrosia
   B. The Holy Grail
   C. The Philosopher's Stone
   D. The Bread of Life

10. Who is Fatima?
    A. She is a woman at the oasis. The boy falls in love with her.
    B. She is the boy's mother that he misses terribly.
    C. She is the crystal merchant's daughter.
    D. She is the boy's camel that he purchased.

Assignment 5
"The boy approached the guard" through "'We'll leave tomorrow before sunrise,' was the alchemist's response."

1. What "omens from the desert" does the boy share with the chieftains of the oasis?
    A. He hears the winds speak to him about the tribal wars.
    B. He sees two hawks fighting and then envisioned the oasis in flames.
    C. He sees a vision of men with swords attacking the oasis.
    D. He uses Urim and Thummim and believes that the oasis is in danger.

2. Who was the boy who saved Egypt through his interpretations of the Pharaoh's dreams?
    A. Abraham
    B. Moses
    C. Joseph
    D. Isaac

3. What decision does the head chieftain make about the boy's visions?
    A. He heeds the boy's warning, yet threatens the boy if they do not come true.
    B. He becomes angry and jails the boy as an enemy spy.
    C. He does not take the boy seriously and ignores him.
    D. He laughs that someone so young could possibly have such visions.

4. What causes a loud, thundering sound and throws the boy to the ground?
    A. A tribe of enemy soldiers arrive on a herd of stampeding camels.
    B. A man dressed in white astride a dark horse demands that the boy answer his questions.
    C. A man dressed in black astride a white horse demands that the boy answer his questions.
    D. A lightning bolt emerges from the sky and struck him down.

5. According to the man on horseback, what is "the quality most essential to understanding the Language of the World?"
    A. Knowledge
    B. Love
    C. Determination
    D. Courage

6. Who is the man on horseback?
   A. It is the alchemist.
   B. It is the chieftian of the oasis.
   C. It is the crystal merchant who decided to go to Mecca after all.
   D. It is the Englishman in disguise.

7. What is the fate of the commander of the enemy battalion?
   A. He is flogged and then released to return to his people as a warning.
   B. He is shot at dawn.
   C. He is given a full pardon and there is peace between the tribes.
   D. He is hanged.

8. What words does the alchemist say that echo those of the old king?
   A. "When a person really desires something, all the universe conspires to help that person to realize his dreams."
   B. "It's not what enters men's mouths that's evil. It's what comes out of their mouths that is."
   C. "Wherever your heart is, there you will find your treasure."
   D. "Love never keeps a man from pursuing his Personal Legend."

9. When riding out into the desert, what does the alchemist instruct the boy to show him?
   A. He tells the boy to show him where there is life in the desert.
   B. He tells the boy to show him where he first saw the omen that led him to warn the chieftain.
   C. He tells the boy to show him how to use Urim and Thummim.
   D. He tells the boy to show him the way to the Pyramids.

Assignment 6
"The boy spent a sleepless night" through "I already know how to turn myself into the wind."

1. Before leaving the oasis, where does the boy go?
    A. He goes to ask the chieftain's blessing for a good journey.
    B. He goes to see the Englishman to thank him for all he has learned.
    C. He goes to see Fatima to tell her that he is leaving the oasis forever.
    D. He goes to see Fatima to say good-bye, and to tell her that he will return for her.

2. What does the desert come to mean for Fatima?
    A. It comes to mean joy because the desert has brought her love, even though it is only meant for a short time.
    B. It comes to mean the hope for the boy's return.
    C. It comes to mean the loss of love.
    D. It came to mean despair because the desert took her love from her.

3. How do the boy and the alchemist find food in the desert?
    A. The alchemist's falcon hunts for food for them.
    B. They pray earnestly each night, and each morning a white covering of manna is on the ground.
    C. Fatima has given them ample supplies to carry with them.
    D. The alchemist has a leather satchel that seems to carry a never-ending supply of food.

4. Why is the boy disappointed when the alchemist writes in the sand what is inscribed on the Emerald Tablet?
    A. The boy expected to learn how to create the Elixir of Life.
    B. It is written in a code the boy does not understand.
    C. The boy thought it would give him the secret to the Language of the World.
    D. The boy expected to learn how to turn any metal into gold.

5. What is it that the alchemist tells the boy that he has to listen to?
    A. He tells the boy he has to listen to the wind.
    B. He tells the boy to listen to the song of the falcon.
    C. He tells the boy he has to listen to his heart.
    D. He tells the boy to listen to the Language of the World in the trees.

6. According to the alchemist, what is worse than suffering?
    A. He says that denying the heart's desire is worse than suffering.
    B. He says that not following one's Personal Legend is worse than suffering.
    C. He says the fear of suffering is worse than the suffering itself.
    D. He says that death is worse than suffering.

7. What is one thing that, according to the alchemist, the boy still needs to know?
    A. He needs to know that the Soul of the World will test him.
    B. He needs to know how to find his way back to the oasis and Fatima.
    C. He needs to know that he must pursue his Personal Legend alone.
    D. He needs to know how to turn ordinary metal into gold.

8. What do the armed tribesmen find in the alchemist's bag?
    A. They find his books on alchemy.
    B. They find a small flask of liquid and a yellow glass egg.
    C. They find the boy's pouch filled with gold.
    D. They find a never-ending supply of food.

9. Why don't the tribesmen take what is in the alchemist's bag?
    A. They think his books are sorcerer's spells, so they refused to touch them.
    B. The alchemist convinces them that the gold is for their tribal leader who needs it to succeed in the wars of the desert.
    C. They believe the food to be bewitched, and so they run in fear.
    D. They don't believe the alchemist when he tells them the truth about the flask and the egg; they merely laugh and go on their way.

10. After they are captured by a tribe, what does the alchemist claim that the boy is able to do?
    A. He says that the boy can create the Elixir of Life and heal the war wounded.
    B. He says that the boy can read omens and can predict the outcome of the war.
    C. He says that the boy can turn himself into the wind and destroy their camp.
    D. He says that the boy can turn any metal into gold, and that the boy will fund their continued war efforts.

Assignment 7
"On the second day, the boy climbed to the top of a cliff" through "They mounted their horses."

1. What does the desert ask the boy to explain to it?
    A. It wants to know the meaning of life.
    B. It wants to know the Language of the World.
    C. It wants to know how to turn lead into gold.
    D. It wants to know what love is.

2. When the desert tells the boy that it cannot help him, whom does it suggest that the boy call on for help?
    A. The desert tells the boy to call on the Wisdom of his Heart.
    B. The desert tells the boy to call on the Language of the World.
    C. The desert tells the boy to call on the wind.
    D. The desert tells the boy to call on the sun.

3. When asked who taught the boy the language of the desert and wind, what is the boy's reply?
    A. He says that the alchemist taught him.
    B. He says that his heart taught him.
    C. He says that experience taught him.
    D. He says that Fatima taught him.

4. Who is the third "person" the boy is told to ask for help from?
    A. He is told to ask for help from the heavens.
    B. He is told to ask for help from his heart.
    C. He is told to ask for help from the wind.
    D. He is told to ask for help from the alchemist.

5. What is the chief's plan for the two men who wanted to end the bet with the boy?
    A. He plans to replace them with the boy and the alchemist.
    B. He plans to execute them for their fears.
    C. He plans to remove them from their positions because they were afraid.
    D. He plans to reward them for not playing into the boy's hand.

6. How does the sun claim to know about love?
    A. The sun claims that it has learned from accidentally destroying what it once loved.
    B. The sun claims that it does not know what love is.
    C. The sun claims that the wind taught it about love.
    D. The sun claims that it has learned that love is about working together.

7. According to the boy, why does alchemy exist?
   A. Alchemy exists to prove that man can create gold from meaningless metals.
   B. Alchemy exists in order to distinguish between those who are searching for the truth and those who are merely greedy.
   C. Alchemy exists so that everyone will search for and find his treasure, and hopefully lead a better life.
   D. Alchemy exists so that everyone can be rich.

8. Why does the wind "scream with delight?"
   A. It screams with delight because the sun's wisdom has its limitations.
   B. It screams with delight because it is turning the boy into the wind.
   C. It screams with delight because it is blowing the tents around the camp.
   D. It screams with delight because the boy knows the Language of the World.

9. What legend did the Arabs recount for generations thereafter?
   A. They retold the stories of the boy who turned himself into the wind and destroyed an entire camp.
   B. They retold the stories of how the boy followed his dreams from Spain to the Great Pyramids of Egypt.
   C. They retold the stories of Joseph and his interpretations of dreams.
   D. They retold the stories of how the alchemist and the boy were able to speak the Language of the World.

10. What feat does the alchemist perform at the monastery?
    A. He creates a flask of the Elixir of Life using a tiny sliver of the Philosopher's Stone.
    B. He heals the sick monk with the Elixir of Life.
    C. He turns lead into gold with the Philosopher's Stone.
    D. He brings a dead monk back to life with the Elixir of Life.

Assignment 8
"I want to tell you a story about dreams" through the Epilogue

1. Describe the dream the alchemist tells to the boy.
    A. The alchemist says that he dreamed that he saw the boy at the Great Pyramids.
    B. The alchemist says that he had dreamed about a boy who would come to him and then turn himself into the wind.
    C. The alchemist reiterates the boy's dream from the sacristy in Spain.
    D. The alchemist tells the dream of a Roman man about his two sons.

2. What did the centurion say that was remembered for all time?
    A. The centurion said that wherever the heart lies, so will your treasure be.
    B. The centurion said that he was not worthy to have a great healer enter his home, but if only the man would say the word, his servant would be healed.
    C. The centurion said that only love can heal a wound.
    D. The centurion said that whenever one has a strong desire, the universe will conspire to make it a reality.

3. What warning does the boy's heart whisper as he is about to climb a large dune?
    A. His heart warns him against greed once he finds his treasure.
    B. His heart warns him to be aware of the place where he is brought to tears.
    C. His heart warns him not to climb the dune because danger lurks behind.
    D. His heart warns him not to trust anyone he meets on the other side of the dune.

4. What does the boy see when he finally reaches the top of the dune?
    A. He sees a beam of light shining on a place in the sand at the foot of the Pyramids.
    B. He sees a band of robbers that have been waiting for him.
    C. He sees the Great Pyramids.
    D. He sees the alchemist smiling brightly, showing him the way to the Pyramids.

5. As the boy wept at the sight that beheld him, what does he notice in the sand?
    A. He notices scarab beetles scuttling in the sand.
    B. He notices that his tears turned into diamonds once they hit the sand.
    C. He notices a snake crawling from a hole and he is reminded of how he had once found life in the desert for the alchemist.
    D. He notices a flower growing out of the sand and believed that it marks the place of his treasure.

6. What does the boy do when he sees the omen?
    A. He begins to dig in the sand with his bare hands.
    B. He weeps harder.
    C. He remembers that the experiences of the journey are more important than reaching his destination, so he prepares to return to Fatima in the oasis.
    D. He becomes afraid the snake will bite him.

7. Describe what happens when the refugees from the tribal wars approach the boy.
    A. The men beat and rob the boy.
    B. The alchemist prevents them from attacking the boy.
    C. They ask him where they can find the alchemist.
    D. They are curious about how to follow their own Personal Legend.

8. What piece of advice does the leader of the refugees give the boy before he leaves?
    A. Never be alone in the desert after dark.
    B. The boy should hurry back to the oasis before Fatima marries another.
    C. Don't bother with dreams; he wasn't stupid enough to go to another country because of a dream.
    D. Don't tell anyone what he knows about the Language of the World.

9. How does the boy finance his journey back to Spain?
    A. He sells sheep.
    B. He sells crystal near the Pyramids.
    C. He works as a caravan leader.
    D. He retrieves the gold that the Alchemist had left for him at the monastery.

10. What does the boy find beneath the sycamore tree in the ruined church?
    A. He finds the Philosopher's Stone that the alchemist left for him.
    B. He finds a bag of diamonds, rubies, and emeralds.
    C. He finds a map that leads directly to buried treasure.
    D. He finds an old conquistador's chest of gold.

ANSWER KEY: STUDY QUESTIONS *The Alchemist*

	1	2	3	4	5	6	7	8
1	A	C	B	A	C	D	D	D
2	D	C	D	C	C	B	C	B
3	A	A	D	C	A	A	B	B
4	D	A	D	C	C	B	A	C
5	C	A	A	B	D	C	C	A
6	A	B	C	C	A	C	D	A
7	A	D	C	A	D	A	C	A
8	D	A	C	C	A	B	A	C
9	B	A	D	C	A	D	A	D
10	D	B	C	A		C	C	D

VOCABULARY WORKSHEETS

VOCABULARY ASSIGNMENT 1 *The Alchemist*

Part I: Using Prior Knowledge and Contextual Clues

Below are the sentences in which the vocabulary words appear in the text. Read the sentence. Use any clues you can find in the sentence combined with your prior knowledge, and write what you think the underlined words mean on the lines provided.

1. The alchemist knew the legend of Narcissus, a youth who knelt beside a lake to contemplate his own beauty.

   _____

2. Dusk was falling as the boy arrived with his herd at an abandoned church. The roof had fallen in long ago, and an enormous sycamore had grown on the spot where the sacristy once had stood.

   _____

3. The merchant was the proprietor of a dry goods shop, and he always demanded that the sheep be sheared in his presence, so that he would not be cheated.

   _____

4. He knew that a few hours from now, with the sun at its zenith, the heat would be so great that he would not be able to lead his flock across the fields.

   _____

5. The horizon was tinged with red, and suddenly the sun appeared.

   _____

6. A shepherd always takes his chances with wolves and with drought, and that's what makes a shepherd's life exciting.

   _____

7. And if the book was irritating, as the old man had said, the boy still had time to change it for another.

   _____

8. The boy didn't know where Salem was, but he didn't want to ask, fearing that he would appear ignorant.

   _____

9. "It prepares your spirit and your will, because there is one great truth on this planet: whoever you are, or whatever it is that you do, when you really want something, its because that desire originated in the soul of the universe."

   _____

10. The boy felt a pang in his heart, thinking about the merchant's daughter.

    _____

The Alchemist Vocabulary Worksheet Assignment 1 Continued

Part II: Determining the Meaning -- Match the vocabulary words to their dictionary definitions.

____ 1. CONTEMPLATE   A. A sudden feeling of mental or emotional distress or longing

____ 2. SACRISTY   B. A slight degree of coloration

____ 3. PROPRIETOR   C. Brought into being; created

____ 4. ZENITH   D. A room in a church housing the sacred vessels and vestments

____ 5. TINGED   E. Exciting to impatience or anger; annoying

____ 6. DROUGHT   F. To consider thoroughly; think fully or deeply about

____ 7. IRRITATING   G. A point on the celestial sphere vertically above a given position

____ 8. IGNORANT   H. A period of dry weather, esp. a long one that is injurious to crops

____ 9. ORIGINATED   I. The owner of a business establishment

____ 10. PANG   J. Lacking in knowledge or training; unlearned

VOCABULARY ASSIGNMENT 2 *The Alchemist*

Part I: Using Prior Knowledge and Contextual Clues

Below are the sentences in which the vocabulary words appear in the text. Read the sentence. Use any clues you can find in the sentence combined with your prior knowledge, and write what you think the underlined words mean on the lines provided.

1. He knew that wind: people called it <u>levanter</u>, because on it the Moors had come from the Levant at the eastern end of the Mediterranean.

   _____

2. "In order to find the treasure, you will have to follow the <u>omens</u>."

   _____

3. "The black signifies 'yes,' and the white 'no.' When you are unable to read the omens, they will help you do so. Always ask an <u>objective</u> question."

   _____

4. He looked to the skies, feeling a bit <u>abashed</u>, and said, "I know it's the vanity of vanities, as you said, my Lord. But an old king sometimes has to take some pride in himself."

   _____

5. The boy felt ill and terribly alone. The <u>infidels</u> had an evil look about them.

   _____

6. The sun began its departure as well. The boy watched it through its <u>trajectory</u> for some time, until it was hidden behind the white houses surrounding the plaza.

   _____

7. He was feeling sorry for himself, and <u>lamenting</u> the fact that his life could have changed so suddenly and so drastically.

   _____

8. He was learning a lot of new things. Some of them were things he had already experienced, and weren't really new, but that he had never <u>perceived</u> them before.

   _____

9. The merchant laughed. "Even if you cleaned my crystal for an entire year ... even if you earned a good <u>commission</u> selling every piece, you would still have to borrow money to get to Egypt."

   _____

The Alchemist Vocabulary Worksheet Assignment 2 Continued

Part II: Determining the Meaning -- Match the vocabulary words to their dictionary definitions.

____ 1. LEVANTER A. Phenomena supposed to portend good or evil; prophetic signs

____ 2. OMENS B. Expressing sorrow or regret

____ 3. OBJECTIVE C. Unbelievers with respect to a particular religion

____ 4. ABASHED D. Became aware of directly through any of the senses

____ 5. INFIDELS E. Ashamed or embarrassed; disconcerted

____ 6. TRAJECTORY F. Path of a projectile or other moving body through space

____ 7. LAMENTING G. Percentage of a sales price allowed to sales representatives for their services

____ 8. PERCEIVED H. Not influenced by personal feelings; based on facts; unbiased

____ 9. COMMISSION I. Strong easterly wind in the Mediterranean

VOCABULARY ASSIGNMENT 3 *The Alchemist*

Part I: Using Prior Knowledge and Contextual Clues

Below are the sentences in which the vocabulary words appear in the text. Read the sentence. Use any clues you can find in the sentence combined with your prior knowledge, and write what you think the underlined words mean on the lines provided.

1. "I don't know anyone around here who would want to cross the desert just to see the Pyramids," said the merchant. "They are just a pile of stones."

   _____

2. "If he makes a buying mistake, it doesn't affect him much. But we two have to live with our mistakes." That's true enough, the boy thought, ruefully.

   _____

3. "The Prophet gave us the Koran, and left us just five obligations to satisfy during our lives."

   _____

4. Anyway, the boy had become happy in his work, and thought all the time about the day when he would disembark at Tarifa as a winner.

   _____

5. It's good I refrained from saying anything to the baker in Tarifa, thought the boy to himself.

   _____

6. For nearly a year, he had been working incessantly, thinking only of putting aside enough money so that he could return to Spain with pride.

   _____

7. But as he held Urim and Thummim in his hand, they had transmitted to him the strength and will of the old king.

   _____

8. He had remembered that one of the crystal merchant's suppliers transported his crystal by means of caravans that crossed the desert.

   _____

9. First he had studied Esperanto, then the world's religions, and now it was alchemy.

   _____

10. The Englishman had been profoundly impressed by the story. But he would never have thought it more than just a myth, had not a friend of his--returning from an archaeological expedition in the desert--told him about an Arab that was possessed of exceptional powers.

    _____

The Alchemist Vocabulary Worksheet Assignment 3 Continued

Part II: Determining the Meaning -- Match the vocabulary words to their dictionary definitions.

____ 1. PYRAMIDS   A. In a manner showing or expressing sorrow or pity; mournfully

____ 2. RUEFULLY   B. Continually; without a break

____ 3. OBLIGATIONS   C. Restrained or held back

____ 4. DISEMBARK   D. To exit a vehicle of transportation

____ 5. REFRAINED   E. Duties

____ 6. INCESSANTLY   F. Passed; transferred

____ 7. TRANSMITTED   G. Medieval philosophy concerned with transmuting common substances into something of value

____ 8. CARAVANS   H. Groups that travel together across the desert or through hostile territory for safety

____ 9. ALCHEMY   I. Excursion, journey, or voyage made for some specific purpose

____ 10. EXPEDITION   J. Pyramid-shaped stone structures in Egypt housing the tombs of great Egyptian leaders

VOCABULARY ASSIGNMENT 4 *The Alchemist*

Part I: Using Prior Knowledge and Contextual Clues

Below are the sentences in which the vocabulary words appear in the text. Read the sentence. Use any clues you can find in the sentence combined with your prior knowledge, and write what you think the underlined words mean on the lines provided.

1. "The desert is a <u>capricious</u> lady, and sometimes she drives men crazy."

    _____

2. "There is no such thing as <u>coincidence</u>," said the Englishman, picking up the conversation where it had been interrupted in the warehouse.

    _____

3. The boy understood <u>intuitively</u> what he meant, even without ever having set foot in the desert before.

    _____

4. "They're not my sheep anymore," he said to himself, without <u>nostalgia</u>. "They must be used to their new shepherd, and have probably already forgotten me. That's good."

    _____

5. At other times, mysterious, hooded men would appear; they were Bedouins who did <u>surveillance</u> along the caravan route.

    _____

6. The travelers adopted the practice of arranging the animals in a circle at night, sleeping together in the center as protection against the <u>nocturnal</u> cold.

    _____

7. "You have a <u>mania</u> for simplifying everything," answered the Englishman, irritated. "Alchemy is a serious discipline."

    _____

8. There were oases throughout the desert, but the tribesmen fought in the desert, leaving oases as places of <u>refuge</u>.

    _____

9. But the Englishman was <u>exultant</u>. They were on the right track.

    _____

10. He had heard people speak of <u>mirages</u>, and had already seen some himself: they were desires that, because of their intensity, materialized over the sands of the desert.

    _____

The Alchemist Vocabulary Worksheet Assignment 4 Continued

Part II: Determining the Meaning -- Match the vocabulary words to their dictionary definitions.

____ 1. CAPRICIOUS   A. Sentimental longing for the happiness of a former place or time
____ 2. COINCIDENCE   B. Shelter or protection from danger or trouble
____ 3. INTUITIVELY   C. Close observations of a person or group
____ 4. NOSTALGIA   D. Of or pertaining to the night
____ 5. SURVEILLANCE   E. Through natural insight; without learning
____ 6. NOCTURNAL   F. Optical illusions in sandy deserts caused by hot air
____ 7. MANIA   G. Subject to whim; impulsive and unpredictable
____ 8. REFUGE   H. Highly elated; jubilant; triumphant
____ 9. EXULTANT   I. Excessive excitement or enthusiasm; craze
____ 10. MIRAGES   J. Seemingly prearranged event that is merely accidental

VOCABULARY ASSIGNMENT 5 *The Alchemist*

Part I: Using Prior Knowledge and Contextual Clues

Below are the sentences in which the vocabulary words appear in the text. Read the sentence. Use any clues you can find in the sentence combined with your prior knowledge, and write what you think the underlined words mean on the lines provided.

1. The ground was covered with the most beautiful carpets he had ever walked upon, and from the top of the structure hung lamps of <u>handwrought</u> gold, each with a lighted candle.

   _____

2. "When the <u>pharaoh</u> dreamed of cows that were thin and cows that were fat, this man I'm speaking of rescued Egypt from famine."

   _____

3. "The Tradition saved Egypt from <u>famine</u> in those days, and made Egyptians the wealthiest of peoples."

   _____

4. The strange horseman drew an enormous, curved sword from a <u>scabbard</u> mounted on his saddle.

   _____

5. "Be careful with your <u>prognostications</u>," said the stranger. "When something is written, there is no way to change it."

   _____

6. When they reached the white tent at the center of Al-Fayoum, they withdrew their <u>scimitars</u> and rifles.

   _____

7. "Isn't wine <u>prohibited</u> here?" the boy asked. "It's not what enters men's mouths that's evil," said the alchemist.

   _____

8. His heart was heavy, and he had been <u>melancholy</u> since the previous night.

   _____

9. "The omens will begin <u>insistently</u> to speak of it, and you'll try to ignore them."

   _____

The Alchemist Vocabulary Worksheet Assignment 5 Continued

Part II: Determining the Meaning -- Match the vocabulary words to their dictionary definitions.

____ 1. HANDWROUGHT   A. Forbidden by authority

____ 2. PHARAOH   B. Made by hand

____ 3. FAMINE   C. Sheath for a sword

____ 4. SCABBARD   D. In a manner compelling attention or notice

____ 5. PROGNOSTICATIONS   E. Gloomy state of mind, esp. when habitual or prolonged

____ 6. SCIMITARS   F. Title of an ancient Egyptian King

____ 7. PROHIBITED   G. Extreme and general scarcity of food, as within a country

____ 8. MELANCHOLY   H. Curved Asian swords with the sharp edge on the convex side

____ 9. INSISTENTLY   I. Forecasts or predictions

VOCABULARY ASSIGNMENT 6 *The Alchemist*

Part I: Using Prior Knowledge and Contextual Clues

Below are the sentences in which the vocabulary words appear in the text. Read the sentence. Use any clues you can find in the sentence combined with your prior knowledge, and write what you think the underlined words mean on the lines provided.

1. The Arab returned to his tent to sleep, proud to have helped the counselor of the oasis, and happy at having enough money to buy himself some sleep.

   _____

2. "Men dream more about coming home than about leaving," the boy said. He was already reaccustomed to the desert's silence.

   _____

3. The desert, with its endless monotony, put him to dreaming.

   _____

4. "In those times, the Master work could be written simply on an emerald. But men began to reject simple things, and to write tracts, interpretations, and philosophical studies.

   _____

5. "But you are in the desert. So immerse yourself in it."

   _____

6. "But my heart is agitated," the boy said. "It has its dreams, it gets emotional, and it's becomes passionate over a woman of the desert."

   _____

7. "Treason is a blow that comes unexpectedly. If you know your heart well, it will never be able to do that to you."

   _____

8. "When I have been truly searching for my treasure, every day has been luminous, because I've known that every hour was a part of the dream that I would find it."

   _____

9. The boy remembered an old proverb from his country. It said that the darkest hour of the night came just before the dawn.

   _____

10. "Whoever swallows that elixir will never be sick again, and a fragment of that stone turns any metal into gold."

    _____

The Alchemist Vocabulary Worksheet Assignment 6 Continued

Part II: Determining the Meaning -- Match the vocabulary words to their dictionary definitions.

____ 1.   OASIS   A. Wearisome uniformity or lack of variety

____ 2.   REACCUSTOMED   B. Excited; disturbed

____ 3.   MONOTONY   C. Short, popular, usually wise saying or precept

____ 4.   TRACTS   D. To involve deeply; soak; sink totally into

____ 5.   IMMERSE   E. Betrayal of a trust or confidence; breach of faith

____ 6.   AGITATED   F. Sweetened mixture of alcohol and water containing medicines

____ 7.   TREASON   G. Brilliant intellectually; enlightening

____ 8.   LUMINOUS   H. Small fertile or green area in a desert region

____ 9.   PROVERB   I. Re-familiarized after having stopped a practice or habit

____ 10. ELIXIR   J. Pamphlets containing a religious or political declaration or appeal

VOCABULARY ASSIGNMENT 7 *The Alchemist*

Part I: Using Prior Knowledge and Contextual Clues

Below are the sentences in which the vocabulary words appear in the text. Read the sentence. Use any clues you can find in the sentence combined with your prior knowledge, and write what you think the underlined words mean on the lines provided.

1. The <u>sentinels</u> allowed him to go; they had already heard about the sorcerer who could turn himself into the wind, and they didn't want to go near him.

   _____

2. There were mountains in the distance. And there were <u>dunes</u>, rocks, and plants that insisted on living where survival seemed impossible.

   _____

3. The wind was a proud being ... It <u>commenced</u> to blow harder, raising the desert sands.

   _____

4. "Each performs its own exact function as a unique being, and everything would be a <u>symphony</u> of peace if the hand that wrote all this had stopped on the fifth day of creation."

   _____

5. "That's what alchemists do. They show that, when we <u>strive</u> to become better than we are, everything around us becomes better, too."

   _____

6. The wind was listening closely, and wanted to tell every corner of the world that the sun's wisdom had its <u>limitations</u>. That it was unable to deal with this boy who spoke the Language of the World.

   _____

7. The tents were being blown from their ties to the earth, and the animals were being freed from their <u>tethers</u>.

   _____

8. Because only the hand understood that it was a larger design that had moved the universe to the point at which six days of creation had <u>evolved</u> into a Master Work.

   _____

9. For generations thereafter, the Arabs recounted the legend of a boy who had turned himself into the wind, almost destroying a military camp, in <u>defiance</u> of the most powerful chief in the desert.

   _____

10. "Thank you," said the boy. "You taught me the Language of the World." "I only <u>invoked</u> what you already knew."

    _____

The Alchemist Vocabulary Worksheet Assignment 7 Continued

Part II: Determining the Meaning -- Match the vocabulary words to their dictionary definitions.

____ 1. SENTINELS A. Daring or bold resistance to authority

____ 2. DUNES B. Harmonious combination of elements

____ 3. COMMENCED C. Exert oneself vigorously; try hard

____ 4. SYMPHONY D. Shortcomings or defects

____ 5. STRIVE E. Ropes, chains, or similar restraints for holding an animal in place

____ 6. LIMITATIONS F. Began

____ 7. TETHERS G. Guards

____ 8. EVOLVED H. Developed gradually

____ 9. DEFIANCE I. Caused, called forth, or brought about

____ 10. INVOKED J. Hills or ridges of wind-blown sand

VOCABULARY ASSIGNMENT 8 *The Alchemist*

Part I: Using Prior Knowledge and Contextual Clues

Below are the sentences in which the vocabulary words appear in the text. Read the sentence. Use any clues you can find in the sentence combined with your prior knowledge, and write what you think the underlined words mean on the lines provided.

1. "The angel touched the man's shoulder, and they were both projected far into the future."

   _____

2. "I knew that my son's poems were immortal," he said to the angel through his tears. "Can you please tell me which of my son's poems these people are repeating?"

   _____

3. "Your son went to serve at a distant place, and became a centurion."

   _____

4. The boy rode along through the desert for several hours, listening avidly to what his heart had to say.

   _____

5. It told of Personal Legend, and of the many men who had wandered in search of distant lands or beautiful women, confronting the people of their times with their preconceived notions.

   _____

6. The boy looked at the sands around him, and saw that, where his tears had fallen, a scarab beetle was scuttling through the sand.

   _____

7. The boy looked at the sands around him, and saw that, where his tears had fallen, a scarab beetle was scuttling through the sand.

   _____

8. He struggled to continue digging as he fought the wind, which often blew the sand back into the excavation. His hands were abraded and exhausted, but he listened to his heart.

   _____

9. "The monk laughed when he saw me come back in tatters."

   _____

The Alchemist Vocabulary Worksheet Assignment 8 Continued

Part II: Determining the Meaning -- Match the vocabulary words to their dictionary definitions.

____ 1. PROJECTED   A. Commander of a century in the Roman army

____ 2. IMMORTAL   B. Thrown forward

____ 3. CENTURION   C. Remembered or celebrated through all time

____ 4. AVIDLY   D. Worn down by scraping or rubbing

____ 5. PRECONCEIVED   E. Forming an opinion before possessing full knowledge

____ 6. SCARAB   F. Type of beetle held sacred by the Ancient Egyptians

____ 7. SCUTTLING   G. Enthusiastically; in a dedicated manner

____ 8. ABRADED   H. Running at a quick pace

____ 9. TATTERS   I. Torn or ragged clothing

VOCABULARY ANSWER KEY - *The Alchemist*

	1	2	3	4	5	6	7	8
1	F	I	J	G	B	H	G	B
2	D	A	A	J	F	I	J	C
3	I	H	E	E	G	A	F	A
4	G	E	D	A	C	J	B	G
5	B	C	C	C	I	D	C	E
6	H	F	B	D	H	B	D	F
7	E	B	F	I	A	E	E	H
8	J	D	H	B	E	G	H	D
9	C	G	G	H	D	C	A	I
10	A		I	F		F	I	

DAILY LESSONS

LESSON ONE

Objectives
1. To analyze the poem "A Dream Deferred" by Langston Hughes to set the theme for the novel *The Alchemist*
2. To familiarize students with the Greek tale of Narcissus in preparation for the allusion in the prologue of *The Alchemist*
3. To be introduced to Paulo Coelho and his novel *The Alchemist*
4. To preview the vocabulary worksheet and study guide questions for reading assignment #1
5. To read reading assignment #1

Activity #1
Tell students to write a journal entry considering the following:

Fully describe a goal or dream that you are working toward. What is the purpose of this goal? What will it help you to achieve after attaining it? What strengths do you possess that will help you along the way?

Ask students to share ideas aloud about their personal dreams/goals. Ask them to think about why they wish to pursue these dreams and how they might feel if they do not follow through.

Read Langston Hughes's poem "a Dream Deferred." Since the poem has gone into public domain, a copy is included in this LitPlan. Have students share their thoughts about the poem and about what happens to dreams that are put off too long.

Activity #2
Give brief notes about the life of Paulo Coelho (see introductory materials for this LitPlan), and discuss how certain aspects of his life might have led him to write a book about spiritual growth and the gaining of self-knowledge.

Activity #3
Distribute the books that the students will use in this unit. Ask them to look at the cover and try to predict what the book might be about. Accept any reasonable response. Then tell students that Paulo Coelho begins the novel with a classical allusion to Greek mythology. Tell students about the Greek myth of Narcissus and attempt to make predictions about how this might tie into Coelho's novel. A brief retelling of the story of Narcissus follows this lesson.

Activity #4
Distribute the materials students will use in this unit. Explain in detail how students are to use these materials.

Study Guides
Students should read the study guide questions for each reading assignment prior to beginning the reading assignment to get a feeling for what events and ideas are important in the section they are about to read. After reading the section, students will (as a class or individually) answer the questions to review the important events and ideas from that section of the book. Students should keep the study guides as study materials for the unit test. **Preview the study questions for Reading Assignment #1 together in class.**

Vocabulary
Prior to each reading assignment, students will do vocabulary work related to the section of the

book they are about to read. Following the completion of the reading of the book, there will be a vocabulary review of all the words used in the vocabulary assignments. Students should keep their vocabulary work as study materials for the unit test. **Do the Vocabulary Worksheet for Reading Assignment #1 together in class.**

Reading Assignment Sheet
You need to fill in the reading assignment sheet to let students know by when their reading has to be completed. You can either write the assignment sheet up on the side blackboard or bulletin board and leave it there for students to see each day, or you can make copies for each student to have. In either case, you should advise students to become very familiar with the reading assignments so they know what is expected of them. Using the edition of the book you are using, add the page numbers that correlate with the reading assignments.

Extra Activities Center
The Unit Resource Materials portion of this LitPlan contains suggestions for an extra library of related books and articles in your classroom as well as crossword and word search puzzles. Make an extra activities center in your room where you will keep these materials for students to use. (Bring the books and articles in from the library and keep several copies of the puzzles on hand.) Explain to students that these materials are available for students to use when they finish reading assignments or other class work early.

Non-fiction Assignment Sheet
Explain to students that they each are to read at least one non-fiction piece from the in-class library at some time during the unit. Students will fill out a Non-fiction Assignment Sheet after completing the reading to help you (the teacher) evaluate their reading experiences and to help the students think about and evaluate their own reading experiences.

Books
Each school has its own rules and regulations regarding student use of school books. Advise students of the procedures that are normal for your school. Preview the book. Look at the covers, front matter, and index.

Activity #5
Students should read Assignment #1 prior to the next class meeting. If time remains in this class, they may begin this assignment.

"A Dream Deferred"
by Langston Hughes

What happens to a dream deferred?

Does it dry up
like a raisin in the sun?
Or fester like a sore--
And then run?
Does it stink like rotten meat?
Or crust and sugar over--
like a syrupy sweet?

Maybe it just sags
like a heavy load.

Or does it explode?

THE STORY OF NARCISSUS

Once upon a time, there was a boy called Narcissus. He was the son of a god and he was very, very handsome. Many women fell in love with him, but he turned them away.
One of the women who loved Narcissus was a nymph called Echo. Echo could not speak properly - she could only repeat what was said to her, so she couldn't tell Narcissus that she loved him.
One day, when Narcissus was walking in the woods with some friends, he became separated from them. He called out "Is anyone here?"
Echo replied "Here, Here".
Echo stepped forward with open arms, wanting to cuddle him.
But Narcissus refused to accept Echo's love. Echo was so upset that she left and hid in a cave, until nothing was left of her, except her voice.
Nemesis, a goddess, found out about this, and she was very angry. She made Narcissus fall in love with himself.
When Narcissus looked at his reflection in a pond one day, he fell in love. He stayed on that spot forever, until he died one day. Where he died a flower grew, and that flower is called a Narcissus.

LESSON TWO

Objectives

1. To review the main events and ideas from Reading Assignment #1
2. To demonstrate reading comprehension through sharing responses to study guide questions
3. To improve oral reading skills through reading a short story, "The Philosopher's Stone" by Hans Christian Andersen
4. To preview the study guide questions and vocabulary for Reading Assignment #2
5. To read Reading Assignment #2

Activity #1

Give students a few minutes to formulate answers for the study guide questions for Reading Assignment #1, and then discuss the answers to the questions in detail. Write the answers on the board or overhead transparency so students can have the correct answers for study purposes.

NOTE: It is a good practice in public speaking and leadership skills for individual students to take charge of leading the discussions of the study questions. Perhaps a different student could go to the front of the class and lead the discussion each day that the study questions are discussed in this unit. Of course, you should guide the discussion when appropriate and try to fill in any gaps students may leave. The study questions could really be handled in a number of different ways, including in small groups with group reports following. Occasionally you may want to use the multiple choice questions as quizzes to check students' reading comprehension. As a short review now and then, students could pair up for the first (or last, if you have time left at the end of a class period) few minutes of class to quiz each other from the study questions. Mix up methods of reviewing the materials and checking comprehension throughout the unit so students don't get bored just answering the questions the same way each day. Variety in methods will also help address the different learning styles of your students. From now on in this unit, the directions will simply say, "Discuss the answers to the study questions in detail as previously directed." You will choose the method of preparation and discussion each day based on what best suits you and your class. While students have their study guides out, preview the questions for Reading Assignment #2.

Activity #2

Tell students to write a journal entry considering the following:

Re-examine your goal/dream that you wrote about yesterday. What fears or weaknesses within you (inner obstacles) need to be overcome in order to attain this goal? Do not reflect upon outside obstacles. What knowledge or skills do you lack at this point that may hinder your progress if not addressed?

These journal entries will aid students in relating to Santiago's own journey.

Activity #3

Ask students if they have ever heard of the Philosopher's Stone or the Elixir of Life. Several may have heard of them through movies or other books. Distribute copies of Hans Christian Andersen's short story "The Philosopher's Stone" and read it aloud. Since the story is in public domain, a copy of the story is included in the LitPlan. You probably know the best way to get readers with your class; pick students at random, ask for volunteers, or use whatever method works best for your group. If you have not yet completed an oral reading evaluation for your students this period, this would be a good opportunity to do so. A form is included with this unit for your convenience.

Activity #4
After reading the tale, have students predict how the idea of the Philosopher's Stone might relate to Paulo Coelho's novel *The Alchemist*.

Activity #5
Remind students to complete vocabulary work and read Reading Assignment #2 prior to the next class meeting.

"The Philosopher's Stone"
by Hans Christian Andersen
(1859)

Far away towards the east, in India, which seemed in those days the world's end, stood the Tree of the Sun; a noble tree, such as we have never seen, and perhaps never may see. The summit of this tree spread itself for miles like an entire forest, each of its smaller branches forming a complete tree. Palms, beech-trees, pines, plane-trees, and various other kinds, which are found in all parts of the world, were here like small branches, shooting forth from the great tree; while the larger boughs, with their knots and curves, formed valleys and hills, clothed with velvety green and covered with flowers. Everywhere it was like a blooming meadow or a lovely garden. Here were birds from all quarters of the world assembled together; birds from the primeval forests of America, from the rose gardens of Damascus, and from the deserts of Africa, in which the elephant and the lion may boast of being the only rulers. Birds from the Polar regions came flying here, and of course the stork and the swallow were not absent. But the birds were not the only living creatures. There were stags, squirrels, antelopes, and hundreds of other beautiful and light-footed animals here found a home.

The summit of the tree was a wide-spreading garden, and in the midst of it, where the green boughs formed a kind of hill, stood a castle of crystal, with a view from it towards every quarter of heaven. Each tower was erected in the form of a lily, and within the stern was a winding staircase, through which one could ascend to the top and step out upon the leaves as upon balconies. The calyx of the flower itself formed a most beautiful, glittering, circular hall, above which no other roof arose than the blue firmament and the sun and stars.

Just as much splendor, but of another kind, appeared below, in the wide halls of the castle. Here, on the walls, were reflected pictures of the world, which represented numerous and varied scenes of everything that took place daily, so that it was useless to read the newspapers, and indeed there were none to be obtained in this spot. All was to be seen in living pictures by those who wished it, but all would have been too much for even the wisest man, and this man dwelt here. His name is very difficult; you would not be able to pronounce it, so it may be omitted. He knew everything that a man on earth can know or imagine. Every invention already in existence or yet to be, was known to him, and much more; still everything on earth has a limit. The wise king Solomon was not half so wise as this man. He could govern the powers of nature and held sway over potent spirits; even Death itself was obliged to give him every morning a list of those who were to die during the day. And King Solomon himself had to die at last, and this fact it was which so often occupied the thoughts of this great man in the castle on the Tree of the Sun. He knew that he also, however high he might tower above other men in wisdom, must one day die. He knew that his children would fade away like the leaves of the forest and become dust. He saw the human race wither and fall like leaves from the tree; he saw new men come to fill their places, but the leaves that fell off never sprouted forth again; they crumbled to dust or were absorbed into other plants.

"What happens to man," asked the wise man of himself, "when touched by the angel of death? What can death be? The body decays, and the soul. Yes; what is the soul, and whither does it go?"

"To eternal life," says the comforting voice of religion.

"But what is this change? Where and how shall we exist?"

"Above; in heaven," answers the pious man; "it is there we hope to go."

"Above!" repeated the wise man, fixing his eyes upon the moon and stars above him. He saw that to this earthly sphere *above* and *below* were constantly changing places, and that the position varied according to the spot on which a man found himself. He knew, also, that even if he ascended to the top of the highest mountain which rears its lofty summit on this earth, the air, which to us seems clear and transparent, would there be dark and cloudy; the sun would have a coppery glow and send forth no rays, and our earth would lie beneath him wrapped in an orange-colored mist. How narrow are the limits which confine the bodily sight, and how little can be seen by the eye of the soul. How little do the wisest among us know of that which is so important to us all.

In the most secret chamber of the castle lay the greatest treasure on earth—the Book of Truth. The wise man had read it through page after page. Every man may read in this book, but only in fragments. To many eyes the characters seem so mixed in confusion that the words cannot be distinguished. On certain pages the writing often appears so pale or so blurred that the page becomes a blank. The wiser a man becomes, the more he will read, and those who are wisest read most.

The wise man knew how to unite the sunlight and the moonlight with the light of reason and the hidden powers of nature; and through this stronger light, many things in the pages were made clear to him. But in the portion of the book entitled "Life after Death" not a single point could he see distinctly. This pained him. Should he never be able here on earth to obtain a light by which everything written in the Book of Truth should become clear to him? Like the wise King Solomon, he understood the language of animals, and could interpret their talk into song; but that made him none the wiser. He found out the nature of plants and metals, and their power in curing diseases and arresting death, but none to destroy death itself. In all created things within his reach he sought the light that should shine upon the certainty of an eternal life, but he found it not. The Book of Truth lay open before him, but, its pages were to him as blank paper. Christianity placed before him in the Bible a promise of eternal life, but he wanted to read it in *his* book, in which nothing on the subject appeared to be written.

He had five children; four sons, educated as the children of such a wise father should be, and a daughter, fair, gentle, and intelligent, but she was blind; yet this deprivation appeared as nothing to her; her father and brothers were outward eyes to her, and a vivid imagination made everything clear to her mental sight. The sons had never gone farther from the castle than the branches of the trees extended, and the sister had scarcely ever left home. They were happy children in that home of their childhood, the beautiful and fragrant Tree of the Sun. Like all children, they loved to hear stories related to them, and their father told them many things which other children would not have understood; but these were as clever as most grownup people are among us. He explained to them what they saw in the pictures of life on the castle walls—the doings of man, and the progress of events in all the lands of the earth; and the sons often expressed a wish that they could be present, and take a part in these great deeds. Then their father told them that in the world there was nothing but toil and difficulty: that it was not quite what it appeared to them, as they looked upon it in their beautiful home. He spoke to them of the true, the beautiful, and the good, and told them that these three held together in the world, and by that union they became crystallized into a precious jewel, clearer than a diamond of the first water—a jewel, whose splendor had a value even in the sight of God, in whose brightness all things are dim. This jewel was called the philosopher's stone. He told them that, by searching, man could attain to a knowledge of the existence of God, and that it was in the power of every man to discover the certainty that such a jewel as the philosopher's stone really existed. This information would have been beyond the perception of other children; but these children understood, and others will learn to comprehend its meaning after a time. They questioned their father about the true, the beautiful, and the good, and he explained it to them in many ways. He told them that God, when He made man out of the dust of the earth, touched His work five times, leaving five intense feelings, which we call the five senses. Through these, the true, the beautiful, and the good are seen, understood, and perceived, and through these they are valued, protected, and encouraged. Five senses have been given mentally and corporeally, inwardly and outwardly, to body and soul.

The children thought deeply on all these things, and meditated upon them day and night. Then the eldest of the brothers dreamt a splendid dream. Strange to say, not only the second brother but also the third and fourth brothers all dreamt exactly the same thing; namely, that each went out into the world to find the philosopher's stone. Each dreamt that he found it, and that, as he rode back on his swift horse, in the morning dawn, over the velvety green meadows, to his home in the castle of his father, that the stone gleamed from his forehead like a beaming light; and threw such a bright radiance upon the pages of the Book of Truth that every word was illuminated which spoke of the life beyond the grave. But the sister had no dream of going out into the wide world; it never entered her mind. Her world was her father's house.

"I shall ride forth into the wide world," said the eldest brother. "I must try what life is like there, as I mix with men. I will practice only the good and true; with these I will protect the beautiful. Much shall be changed for the better while I am there."

Now these thoughts were great and daring, as our thoughts generally are at home, before we have gone out into the world, and encountered its storms and tempests, its thorns and its thistles. In him, and in all his brothers, the five senses were highly cultivated, inwardly and outwardly; but each of them had one sense which in keenness and development surpassed the other four. In the case of the eldest, this pre-eminent sense was *sight*, which he hoped would be of special service. He had eyes for all times and all people; eyes that could discover in the depths of the earth hidden treasures, and look into the hearts of men, as through a pane of glass; he could read more than is often seen on the cheek that blushes or grows pale, in the eye that droops or smiles. Stags and antelopes accompanied him to the western boundary of his home, and there he found the wild swans. These he followed, and found himself far away in the north, far from the land of his father, which extended eastward to the ends of the earth. How he opened his eyes with astonishment! How many things were to be seen here! and so different to the mere representation of pictures such as those in his father's house. At first he nearly lost his eyes in astonishment at the rubbish and mockery brought forward to represent the beautiful; but he kept his eyes, and soon found full employment for them. He wished to go thoroughly and honestly to work in his endeavor to understand the true, the beautiful, and the good. But how were they represented in the world? He observed that the wreath which rightly belonged to the beautiful was often given the hideous; that the good was often passed by unnoticed, while mediocrity was applauded, when it should have been hissed. People look at the dress, not at the wearer; thought more of a name than of doing their duty; and trusted more to reputation than to real service. It was everywhere the same.

"I see I must make a regular attack on these things," said he; and he accordingly did not spare them. But while looking for the truth, came the evil one, the father of lies, to intercept him. Gladly would the fiend have plucked out the eyes of this *Seer*, but that would have been a too straightforward path for him; he works more cunningly. He allowed the young man to seek for, and discover, the beautiful and the good; but while he was contemplating them, the evil spirit blew one mote after another into each of his eyes; and such a proceeding would injure the strongest sight. Then he blew upon the motes, and they became beams, so that the clearness of his sight was gone, and the *Seer* was like a blind man in the world, and had no longer any faith in it. He had lost his good opinion of the world, as well as of himself; and when a man gives up the world, and himself too, it is all over with him.

"All over," said the wild swan, who flew across the sea to the east.

"All over," twittered the swallows, who were also flying eastward towards the Tree of the Sun. It was no good news which they carried home.

"I think the *Seer* has been badly served," said the second brother, "but the *Hearer* may be more successful."

This one possessed the sense of *hearing* to a very high degree: so acute was this sense, that it was said he could hear the grass grow. He took a fond leave of all at home, and rode away, provided with good abilities and good intentions. The swallows escorted him, and he followed the swans till he found himself out in the world, and far away from home. But he soon discovered that one may have too much of a good thing. His hearing was too fine. He not only heard the grass grow, but could hear every man's heart beat, whether in sorrow or in joy. The whole world was to him like a clockmaker's great workshop, in which all the clocks were going "tick, tick," and all the turret clocks striking "ding, dong." It was unbearable. For a long time his ears endured it, but at last all the noise and tumult became too much for one man to bear.

There were rascally boys of sixty years old—for years do not alone make a man—who raised a tumult, which might have made the *Hearer* laugh, but for the applause which followed, echoing through every street and house, and was even heard in country roads. Falsehood thrust itself forward and played the hypocrite; the bells on the fool's cap jingled, and declared they were church-bells, and the noise became so bad for the *Hearer* that he thrust his fingers into his ears. Still, he could hear false notes and bad singing, gossip and idle words, scandal and slander, groaning and moaning, without and within. "Heaven help us!" He thrust his fingers farther and farther into his ears, till at last the drums burst. And now he could hear nothing more of the true, the beautiful, and the good; for his hearing was to have been the means by which he hoped to acquire his knowledge. He became silent and suspicious, and at last trusted no one, not even himself, and no longer hoping to find and bring home the costly jewel, he gave it up, and gave himself up too, which was worse than all.

The birds in their flight towards the east, carried the tidings, and the news reached the castle in the Tree of the Sun.

"*I* will try now," said the third brother; "I have a keen *nose.*" Now that was not a very elegant expression, but it was his way, and we must take him as he was. He had a cheerful temper, and was, besides, a real poet; he could make many things appear poetical, by the way in which he spoke of them, and ideas struck him long before they occurred to the minds of others. "I can smell," he would say; and he attributed to the sense of smelling, which he possessed in a high degree, a great power in the region of the beautiful. "I can smell," he would say, "and many places are fragrant or beautiful according to the taste of the frequenters. One man feels at home in the atmosphere of the tavern, among the flaring tallow candles, and when the smell of spirits mingles with the fumes of bad tobacco. Another prefers sitting amidst the overpowering scent of jasmine, or perfuming himself with scented olive oil. This man seeks the fresh sea breeze, while that one climbs the lofty mountain-top, to look down upon the busy life in miniature beneath him."

As he spoke in this way, it seemed as if he had already been out in the world, as if he had already known and associated with man. But this experience was intuitive—it was the poetry within him, a gift from Heaven bestowed on him in his cradle. He bade farewell to his parental roof in the Tree of the Sun, and departed on foot, from the pleasant scenes that surrounded his home. Arrived at its confines, he mounted on the back of an ostrich, which runs faster than a horse, and afterwards, when he fell in with the wild swans, he swung himself on the strongest of them, for he loved change, and away he flew over the sea to distant lands, where there were great forests, deep lakes, lofty mountains, and proud cities. Wherever he came it seemed as if sunshine traveled with him across the fields, for every flower, every bush, exhaled a renewed fragrance, as if conscious that a friend and protector was near; one who understood them, and knew their value. The stunted rose-bush shot forth twigs, unfolded its leaves, and bore the most beautiful roses; every one could see it, and even the black, slimy wood-snail noticed its beauty. "I will give my seal to the flower," said the snail, "I have trailed my slime upon it, I can do no more."

"Thus it always fares with the beautiful in this world," said the poet. And he made a song upon it, and sung it after his own fashion, but nobody listened. Then he gave a drummer two-pence and a peacock's feather, and composed a song for the drum, and the drummer beat it through the streets of the town, and when the people heard it they said, "That is a capital tune." The poet wrote many songs about the true, the beautiful, and the good. His songs were listened to in the tavern, where the tallow candles flared, in the fresh clover field, in the forest, and on the high-seas; and it appeared as if this brother was to be more fortunate than the other two.

But the evil spirit was angry at this, so he set to work with soot and incense, which he can mix so artfully as to confuse an angel, and how much more easily a poor poet. The evil one knew how to manage such people. He so completely surrounded the poet with incense that the man lost his head, forgot his mission and his home, and at last lost himself and vanished in smoke.

But when the little birds heard of it, they mourned, and for three days they sang not one song. The black wood-snail became blacker still; not for grief, but for envy. "They should have offered me incense," he said, "for it was I who gave him the idea of the most famous of his songs—the drum song of 'The Way of the World;' and it was I who spat at the rose; I can bring a witness to that fact."

But no tidings of all this reached the poet's home in India. The birds had all been silent for three days, and when the time of mourning was over, so deep had been their grief, that they had forgotten for whom they wept. Such is the way of the world.

"Now I must go out into the world, and disappear like the rest," said the fourth brother. He was as good-tempered as the third, but no poet, though he could be witty.

The two eldest had filled the castle with joyfulness, and now the last brightness was going away. Sight and hearing have always been considered two of the chief senses among men, and those which they wish to keep bright; the other senses are looked upon as of less importance.

But the younger son had a different opinion; he had cultivated his taste in every way, and taste is very powerful. It rules over what goes into the mouth, as well as over all which is presented to the mind; and, consequently, this brother took upon himself to *taste* everything stored up in bottles or jars; this he called the rough part of his work. Every man's mind was to him as a vessel in which something was concocting; every land a kind of mental kitchen. "There are no delicacies here," he said; so he wished to go out into the world to find something delicate to suit his taste. "Perhaps fortune may be more favorable to me than it was to my brothers. I shall start on my travels, but what conveyance shall I choose? Are air balloons invented yet?" he asked of his father, who knew of all inventions that had been made, or would be made.

Air balloons had not then been invented, nor steam-ships, nor railways.

"Good," said he; "then I shall choose an air balloon; my father knows how they are to be made and guided. Nobody has invented one yet, and the people will believe that it is an aerial phantom. When I have done with the balloon I shall burn it, and for this purpose, you must give me a few pieces of another invention, which will come next; I mean a few chemical matches."

He obtained what he wanted, and flew away. The birds accompanied him farther than they had the other brothers. They were curious to know how this flight would end. Many more of them came swooping down; they thought it must be some new bird, and he soon had a goodly company of followers. They came in clouds till the air became darkened with birds as it was with the cloud of locusts over the land of Egypt.

And now he was out in the wide world. The balloon descended over one of the greatest cities, and the aeronaut took up his station at the highest point, on the church steeple. The balloon rose again into the air, which it ought not to have done; what became of it is not known, neither is it of any consequence, for balloons had not then been invented.

There he sat on the church steeple. The birds no longer hovered over him; they had got tired of him, and he was tired of them. All the chimneys in the town were smoking.

"There are altars erected to my honor," said the wind, who wished to say something agreeable to him as he sat there boldly looking down upon the people in the street. There was one stepping along, proud of his purse; another, of the key he carried behind him, though he had nothing to lock up; another took a pride in his moth-eaten coat; and another, in his mortified body. "Vanity, all vanity!" he exclaimed. "I must go down there by-and-by, and touch and taste; but I shall sit here a little while longer, for the wind blows pleasantly at my back. I shall remain here as long as the wind blows, and enjoy a little rest. It is comfortable to sleep late in the morning when one had a great deal to do," said the sluggard; "so I shall stop here as long as the wind blows, for it pleases me."

And there he stayed. But as he was sitting on the weather-cock of the steeple, which kept turning round and round with him, he was under the false impression that the same wind still blew, and that he could stay where he was without expense.

But in India, in the castle on the Tree of the Sun, all was solitary and still, since the brothers had gone away one after the other.

"Nothing goes well with them," said the father; "they will never bring the glittering jewel home, it is not made for me; they are all dead and gone." Then he bent down over the Book of Truth, and gazed on the page on which he should have read of the life after death, but for him there was nothing to be read or learned upon it.

His blind daughter was his consolation and joy; she clung to him with sincere affection, and for the sake of his happiness and peace she wished the costly jewel could be found and brought home.

With longing tenderness she thought of her brothers. Where were they? Where did they live? How she wished she might dream of them; but it was strange that not even in dreams could she be brought near to them. But at last one night she dreamt that she heard the voices of her brothers calling to her from the distant world, and she could not refrain herself, but went out to them, and yet it seemed in her dream that she still remained in her father's house. She did not *see* her brothers, but she *felt* as it were a fire burning in her hand, which, however, did not hurt her, for it was the jewel she was bringing to her father. When she awoke she thought for a moment that she still held the stone, but she only grasped the knob of her distaff.

During the long evenings she had spun constantly, and round the distaff were woven threads finer than the web of a spider; human eyes could never have distinguished these threads when separated from each other. But she had wetted them with her tears, and the twist was as strong as a cable. She rose with the impression that her dream must be a reality, and her resolution was taken.

It was still night, and her father slept; she pressed a kiss upon his hand, and then took her distaff and fastened the end of the thread to her father's house. But for this, blind as she was, she would never have found her way home again; to this thread she must hold fast, and trust not to others or even to herself. From the Tree of the Sun she broke four leaves; which she gave up to the wind and the weather, that they might be carried to her brothers as letters and a greeting, in case she did not meet them in the wide world. Poor blind child, what would become of her in those distant regions? But she had the invisible thread, to which she could hold fast; and she possessed a gift which all the others lacked. This was a determination to throw herself entirely into whatever she undertook, and it made her feel as if she had eyes even at the tips of her fingers, and could hear down into her very heart. Quietly she went forth into the noisy, bustling, wonderful world, and wherever she went the skies grew bright, and she felt the warm sunbeam, and a rainbow above in the blue heavens seemed to span the dark world. She heard the song of the birds, and smelt the scent of the orange groves and apple orchards so strongly that she seemed to taste it. Soft tones and charming songs reached her ear, as well as harsh sounds and rough words—thoughts and opinions in strange contradiction to each other. Into the deepest recesses of her heart penetrated the echoes of human thoughts and feelings. Now she heard the following words sadly sung,—

"Life is a shadow that flits away
  In a night of darkness and woe."

But then would follow brighter thoughts:
"Life has the rose's sweet perfume

With sunshine, light, and joy."

And if one stanza sounded painfully—
"Each mortal thinks of himself alone,
Is a truth, alas, too clearly known;"
Then, on the other hand, came the answer—
"Love, like a mighty flowing stream,
Fills every heart with its radiant gleam."
She heard, indeed, such words as these—
"In the pretty turmoil here below,
All is a vain and paltry show."
Then came also words of comfort—
"Great and good are the actions done
By many whose worth is never known."
And if sometimes the mocking strain reached her—
"Why not join in the jesting cry
That contemns all gifts from the throne on high?"
In the blind girl's heart a stronger voice repeated—
"To trust in thyself and God is best,
In His holy will forever to rest."
But the evil spirit could not see this and remain contented. He has more cleverness than ten thousand men, and he found means to compass his end. He betook himself to the marsh, and collected a few little bubbles of stagnant water. Then he uttered over them the echoes of lying words that they might become strong. He mixed up together songs of praise with lying epitaphs, as many as he could find, boiled them in tears shed by envy; put upon them rouge, which he had scraped from faded cheeks, and from these he produced a maiden, in form and appearance like the blind girl, the angel of completeness, as men called her. The evil one's plot was successful. The world knew not which was the true, and indeed how should the world know?
"To trust in thyself and God is best,
In his Holy will forever to rest."

So sung the blind girl in full faith. She had entrusted the four green leaves from the Tree of the Sun to the winds, as letters of greeting to her brothers, and she had full confidence that the leaves would reach them. She fully believed that the jewel which outshines all the glories of the world would yet be found, and that upon the forehead of humanity it would glitter even in the castle of her father. "Even in my father's house," she repeated. "Yes, the place in which this jewel is to be found is earth, and I shall bring more than the promise of it with me. I feel it glow and swell more and more in my closed hand. Every grain of truth which the keen wind carried up and whirled towards me I caught and treasured. I allowed it to be penetrated with the fragrance of the beautiful, of which there is so much in the world, even for the blind. I took the beatings of a heart engaged in a good action, and added them to my treasure. All that I can bring is but dust; still, it is a part of the jewel we seek, and there is plenty, my hand is quite full of it."
She soon found herself again at home; carried thither in a flight of thought, never having loosened her hold of the invisible thread fastened to her father's house. As she stretched out her hand to her father, the powers of evil dashed with the fury of a hurricane over the Tree of the Sun; a blast of wind rushed through the open doors, and into the sanctuary, where lay the Book of Truth.

"It will be blown to dust by the wind," said the father, as he seized the open hand she held towards him.

"No," she replied, with quiet confidence, "it is indestructible. I feel its beam warming my very soul."

Then her father observed that a dazzling flame gleamed from the white page on which the shining dust had passed from her hand. It was there to prove the certainty of eternal life, and on the book glowed one shining word, and only one, the word BELIEVE. And soon the four brothers were again with the father and daughter. When the green leaf from home fell on the bosom of each, a longing had seized them to return. They had arrived, accompanied by the birds of passage, the stag, the antelope, and all the creatures of the forest who wished to take part in their joy.

We have often seen, when a sunbeam burst through a crack in the door into a dusty room, how a whirling column of dust seems to circle round. But this was not poor, insignificant, common dust, which the blind girl had brought; even the rainbow's colors are dim when compared with the beauty which shone from the page on which it had fallen. The beaming word BELIEVE, from every grain of truth, had the brightness of the beautiful and the good, more bright than the mighty pillar of flame that led Moses and the children of Israel to the land of Canaan, and from the word BELIEVE arose the bridge of hope, reaching even to the immeasurable Love in the realms of the infinite.

ORAL READING EVALUATION- *The Alchemist*

Name _____ Class____ Date _____

SKILL	EXCELLENT	GOOD	AVERAGE	FAIR	POOR
Fluency	5	4	3	2	1
Clarity	5	4	3	2	1
Audibility	5	4	3	2	1
Pronunciation	5	4	3	2	1
_____	5	4	3	2	1
_____	5	4	3	2	1

Total _____   Grade _____

Comments:

LESSON THREE

<u>Objectives</u>
1. To review the main events, ideas, and vocabulary for Reading Assignment #2
2. To demonstrate reading comprehension through taking a quiz
3. To practice writing skills through planning on how to write an essay
4. To preview the study guide questions and vocabulary for Reading Assignment #3
5. To read Reading Assignment #3

<u>Activity #1</u>
Discuss the answers to the study questions for Reading Assignment #2 as previously directed. While students have their study guides out, preview the questions for Reading Assignment #3.

<u>Activity #2</u>
Discuss or post the answers to the vocabulary for Assignment #2 so students have the correct answers for study purposes.

<u>Activity #3</u>
Quiz- Distribute quizzes for Reading Assignments #1 and #2 and give students about 10 minutes to complete them.

<u>Activity #4</u>
Tell students to write a journal entry considering the following:

What mentor/helper do you have on your journey to guide you? What skills/talents does this person possess that you would like to acquire within yourself? What tools or gifts have you been given that will help you along the way? What strengths do you have available within you?

<u>Activity #5</u>
Distribute Writing Assignment #1 and discuss the directions in detail. Ask students to make their independent reading choices by the next class meeting.

<u>Activity #6</u>
Go to the library/media center so students can begin the research portion of the paper.

<u>Activity #7</u>
Remind students to complete vocabulary work and read Reading Assignment #3 prior to the next class meeting.

WRITING ASSIGNMENT #1 *The Alchemist*

PROMPT
You are reading *The Alchemist* by Paulo Coelho, which is about a boy who gives up everything he has in order to follow his dream. Along the way, he will meet an alchemist who knows the secrets of the Philosopher's Stone and the Elixir of Life. You will be researching the legends of the Philosopher's Stone and the Elixir of Life in order to gain insights into the mystical power they are presumed to possess. After gaining a clearer understanding of this power, you will then select one of the following works that also involve these legendary elements and reflect on how the characters use, or intend to use, the mystical powers of alchemy. Are the powers of alchemy used appropriately, or does the desire for some other sort of power overshadow the character's judgement? You will be required to give a presentation about the work you read and its correlation to the topic at the end of the unit.

PREWRITING
Part I: Research the legends surrounding the Philosopher's Stone and the Elixir of Life. Take notes from articles from the library or the Internet that may prove helpful in supporting your ideas throughout this project.

Part II: Select one of the following works:
 Harry Potter and the Sorcerer's Stone by J.K. Rowling
 Indiana Jones and the Philosopher's Stone by Max McCoy
 Frankenstein by Mary Wollstonecraft Shelley
 Parsifal by Cretien de Troyes
 Reainmator by H. P. Lovecraft

As you read, make copious notes about the references to the Philosopher's Stone or the Elixir of Life as revealed in your research. You should also create character sketches for both the protagonist and the antagonist that outline both positive and negative character traits.

DRAFTING
Your introduction should include a discussion of both the Philosopher's Stone and the Elixir of Life based on your research. You also need to refer to the work you have selected to analyze for this assignment. Your thesis statement should reveal whether or not the character attempts to use the powers of alchemy appropriately or if he/she was driven by some other force. Use your character sketch notes (taken during your reading) to help you. For the body, be sure to write at least two paragraphs demonstrating how the character of your selected work reflects the main idea of your thesis. Incorporate at least two quotations from both the work itself and from the articles you'd printed out as support. Finally, make connections to Paulo Coelho's treatment of the topic of alchemy in his novel, *The Alchemist*. You are required to correctly use five vocabulary words from the unit in your essay.

PROMPT
When you finish the rough draft of your paper, ask a person whose opinion you trust to read it. After reading your rough draft, he/she should tell you what he/she liked best about your work, which parts were difficult to understand, and ways in which your work could be improved. Reread your paper considering your critic's comments, and make the corrections you think are necessary.

PROOFREADING
Do a final proofreading of your paper, double-checking your grammar, spelling, organization, and the clarity of your ideas.

Presentation Worksheet *The Alchemist*

Name_____

Brief synopsis of the work selected:

Character sketch of protagonist:

Character sketch of antagonist:

How the Philosopher's Stone and/or the Elixir of Life relates to the work:

How the work relates to *The Alchemist:*

WRITING EVALUATION FORM - *The Alchemist*

Name _____ Date _____

Grade _____

Circle One For Each Item:

Grammar:	correct errors noted on paper
Spelling:	correct errors noted on paper
Punctuation:	correct errors noted on paper
Legibility:	excellent good fair poor
_____	excellent good fair poor
_____	excellent good fair poor

Strengths:

Weaknesses:

Comments/Suggestions:

LESSON FOUR

Objectives
1. To review the main events, ideas, and vocabulary for Reading Assignment #3
2. To read a non-fiction article related to the topic of divination and relate it to *The Alchemist*
3. To practice research skills in the library/media center
4. To preview the study guide questions and vocabulary for Reading Assignment #4
5. To read Reading Assignment #4

Activity #1
Discuss the answers to the study questions for Assignment #3 as previously directed. While students have their study questions out, preview the study questions for Reading Assignment #4.

Activity #2
Discuss or post the answers to the vocabulary for Assignment #3 so students have the correct answers for study purposes.

Activity #3
Tell students to write a journal entry considering this question:

What outside obstacles must be faced in order to achieve your goal? How will you successfully overcome these obstacles while still maintaining your true sense of self? How can you honestly bring about change without compromising your own principles or values?

Activity #4
Distribute the non-fiction reading assignment and discuss the directions in detail. Each student will complete the Non-fiction Reading Assignment Sheet based on his/her particular articles he/she finds in the library/media center.

Activity #5
Remind students to complete the vocabulary work and read Reading Assignment #4 prior to the next class meeting.

NON-FICTION READING ASSIGNMENT *The Alchemist*

Throughout the novel *The Alchemist,* Paulo Coelho's protagonist Santiago is instructed to follow omens in order to figure out which course he is destined to take. An omen is defined as "a sign of something, either good or bad, that is to come." The boy, Santiago, is given a pair of stones known as Urim and Thummim to use as a divination tool. Divination is a way of attempting to know the future.

For your task, you will research one specific type of divination from a list of various types that have been used throughout history. How does the particular type of divination work, based on your findings? What function does the use of divination play for those faced with indecision? How does its use play a role in *The Alchemist*?

Complete the accompanying worksheet after reading your articles about the type of divination you have selected. You will be sharing your findings in class in a few days.

Choose from the following:
- Tarot cards
- I ching
- Runes
- Scrying
- Tea leaves
- Bibliomancy

NON-FICTION ASSIGNMENT SHEET
(To be completed after reading the required non-fiction article)

Name _____ Date _____

Title of Non-fiction Read_____

Written By _____ Publication Date _____

I. Factual Summary: Write a short summary of the piece you read.

II. Vocabulary
    1. With which vocabulary words in the piece did you encounter some degree of difficulty?

    2. How did you resolve your lack of understanding with these words?

III. Interpretation: What was the main point the author wanted you to get from reading his work?

IV. Criticism
    1. With which points of the piece did you agree or find easy to accept? Why?

    2. With which points of the piece did you disagree or find difficult to believe? Why?

V. Personal Response: What do you think about this piece? OR How does this piece influence your ideas/thinking?

LESSON FIVE

Objectives
1. To review the main events, ideas, and vocabulary for Reading Assignment #4
2. To demonstrate reading comprehension through taking a quiz
3. To demonstrate character analysis skills through the creation of a poster
4. To work in co-operative groups
5. To practice note-taking skills
6. To practice public speaking skills through presentation of a poster
7. To preview the study guide questions and vocabulary for Reading Assignment #5
8. To read Reading Assignment #5

Activity #1
Discuss the answers to the study questions for Assignment #4 as previously directed. While students have their study guides out, preview the study questions for Reading Assignment #5.

Activity #2
Discuss or post the answers to the vocabulary for Assignment #4 so students have the correct answers for study purposes.

Activity #3
Quiz- Distribute quizzes for Reading Assignment #3 and #4 and give students about 10 minutes to complete them.

Activity #4
Tell students to write a journal entry considering these questions:

Once you have obtained your present goal, what will you do with your new knowledge/skill/gift? How do you suppose your life will be different once you have succeeded at this task? How may it benefit your life? How might it benefit the lives of others?

Activity #5
Divide the class into six groups. Assign each group one of the following: Santiago, the King of Salem, the gypsy woman, the crystal merchant, Fatima, the Englishman. Have each group create a characterization poster that includes:
-- A picture of the character based on Paulo Coelho's descriptions
-- Three positive character traits based on textual events (cite lines and page numbers as support)
-- Two negative character traits based on textual events (cite lines and page numbers as support)
When groups are finished, have each present its poster and its analysis of the character. Students not presenting should take notes about each character as they are presented.

Activity #6
Remind students to do vocabulary work and read Reading Assignment #5 prior to the next class meeting.

LESSON SIX

<u>Objectives</u>
1. To review the main events, ideas, and vocabulary for Reading Assignment #5
2. To check students' non-fiction reading assignments
3. To practice speaking skills through the sharing of non-fiction findings
4. To practice note-taking skills
5. To work as a large group to create a map
6. To preview the study guide questions and vocabulary for Reading Assignment #6
7. To read Reading Assignment #6

<u>Activity #1</u>
Discuss the answers to the study questions for Assignment #5 as previously directed. While students have their study guides out, preview the study questions for Reading Assignment #6.

<u>Activity #2</u>
Discuss or post the answers to the vocabulary for Assignment #5 so students have the correct answers for study purposes.

<u>Activity #3</u>
Tell students to write a journal entry considering the following:

Imagine that you have NOT been able to attain your chosen goal. How might this affect your overall journey? What adjustments might need to be made in the event that the original goal set is unobtainable? Will the possibility of falling short of attaining your Ultimate Boon change the way you view yourself, or the way you believe others will perceive you? Do you believe that the effort put into the journey will have been wasted? Or do you believe that learning from mistakes/failure is part of the learning process? Explain your answer in depth.

<u>Activity #4</u>
Allow students to share findings from the non-fiction assignments. Ask each student to give a <u>brief</u> report. Be sure to discuss how the use of divination relates to *The Alchemist*. Students listening to others should take notes.

<u>Activity #5</u>
Get a very large piece of paper (perhaps your art department can help with this). As a group, discuss the journey of Santiago up to this point. Using a geographic map as a guide, have students work together to draw a large map that includes Spain and Northern Africa. Students may draw dotted lines to outline Santiago's journey, as well as illustrate it using details from the novel. Hang the finished map on the wall where it can be easily added to as the novel progresses.

<u>Activity #6</u>
Remind students to do vocabulary work and read Reading Assignment #6 prior to the next class meeting.

LESSON SEVEN

<u>Objectives</u>
1. To review the main events, ideas, and vocabulary for Reading Assignment #6
2. To demonstrate reading comprehension through taking a quiz
3. To begin Writing Assignment #2
4. To preview the study guide questions and vocabulary for Reading Assignment #7
5. To read Reading Assignment #7

<u>Activity #1</u>
Discuss the answers to the study questions for Reading Assignment #6 as previously directed. While students have their study guides out, preview the study questions for Reading Assignment #7.

<u>Activity #2</u>
Discuss or post the answers to the vocabulary for Assignment #6 so students have the correct answers for study purposes.

<u>Activity #3</u>
Quiz- Distribute quizzes for Reading Assignments #5 and #6, and give students about 10 minutes to complete them.

<u>Activity #4</u>
Distribute Writing Assignment #2 and discuss the directions in detail. Tell students to brainstorm with a partner and then begin planning and writing their journal entries.

<u>Activity #5</u>
Remind students to do vocabulary work and read Reading Assignment #7 for next class.

WRITING ASSIGNMENT #2 *The Alchemist*

PROMPT
While Paulo Coelho's novel *The Alchemist* is written in third person, the reader is primarily introduced to the thoughts and feelings of the shepherd boy, Santiago. During the boy's travels, he comes in contact with others who influence his journey, whether they realize it or not. You will select two of these characters from a list provided and create a journal for each. Your journals will consist of four separate entries that will be outlined for you. Present them in a creative way (try to make them realistic-looking).

PREWRITING
Select two of the following seven characters and create a series of four believable journal entries for each choice. Three prompts are provided; you are to create a believable fourth based on some event from the novel.

- The Gypsy woman
  * Her reaction to her interpretation of the boy's dream
  * Her reaction to learning that the boy has left town
  * Her reaction when the boy fulfills his promise to her
- The King of Salem
  * His reaction to his meeting with the boy
  * His reaction upon receiving the sheep
  * His reaction to learning that the boy has left town
- The Thief
  * His reaction to meeting with the boy
  * His reaction to carrying out his plot to rob the boy
  * His reaction to learning that the boy was working at the Crystal Shop
- The Crystal Salesman
  * His reaction to the boy cleaning the crystal
  * His reaction to the boy working in the shop
  * His reaction to learning the boy has left town
- Fatima
  * Her reaction after first meeting the boy
  * Her reaction to his telling her he loves her
  * Her reaction to the boy's return
- The Englishman
  * His reaction to his meeting with the boy
  * His observations of the world (in place of reading his books)
  * His reaction to meeting the alchemist
- The Alchemist
  * His reaction to meeting the boy
  * His reaction to the boy turning into the wind
  * His response to the boy's reaction at seeing him turn lead to gold

DRAFTING
Your entries must have a believable voice for each character, as well as an accurate account of events as they would be known by the character. They must be written in first person and be at least seventy-five words in length each. You are required to correctly use five vocabulary words from the unit within your journal entries.

PROMPT
When you finish the rough draft of your journal, ask someone whose opinion you trust to read it. After reading your rough draft, he/she should tell you what he/she liked best about your work, which parts were difficult to understand, and ways in which your work could be improved.

Reread your paper considering your critic's comments, and make the corrections you think are necessary.

PROOFREADING
Do a final proofreading of your paper double-checking your grammar, spelling, organization, and the clarity of your ideas.

LESSON EIGHT

Objectives
1. To review the main events, ideas, and vocabulary for Reading Assignment #7
2. To practice oral reading skills
3. To preview the study guide questions and vocabulary for Reading Assignment #8
4. To read Reading Assignment #8

Activity #1
Discuss the answers to the study questions for Reading Assignment #7 as previously directed. While students have their study guides out, preview study questions for Reading Assignment #8.

Activity #2
Discuss or post the answers to the vocabulary for Assignment #7 so students have the correct answers for study purposes.

Activity #3
Do the vocabulary worksheet for Reading Assignment #8 orally together in class.

Activity #4
Read Reading Assignment #8 orally in class. You probably know the best way to get readers; pick students at random, ask for volunteers, or use whatever method works best for your group. If you have not yet completed oral reading evaluations, this would be a good opportunity to do so.

LESSON NINE

Objectives
1. To review the main events, ideas, and vocabulary for Reading Assignment #8
2. To demonstrate reading comprehension through taking a quiz
3. To analyze Biblical allusions in *The Alchemist*
4. To improve co-operative learning skills through working in groups

Activity #1
Discuss the answers to the study questions for Reading Assignment #8 as previously directed.

Activity #2
Discuss or post the answers to the vocabulary for Assignment #8 so students have the correct answers for study purposes.

Activity #3
Quiz- Distribute quizzes for Reading Assignments #7 and #8 and give students about 10 minutes to complete them.

Activity #4
Divide the class into five groups, one for each of the following Biblical allusions found in *The Alchemist*. Go to the library/media center so that students may access the internet to find the scriptures listed.

Melchizedek (page 19)
"My name is Melchizedek," said the old man. "How many sheep do you have?"
Hebrews 5:6
Hebrews 5:10
Hebrews 7:2
Hebrews 7:3
Hebrews 7:15
Genesis 14:18

The Roman Centurion (page 158)
"Your son went to serve at a distant place, and became a centurion."
Luke 7: 1-10
Matthew 8: 5-13

Joseph of Egypt (page 107)
"... this man I am speaking of rescued Egypt from famine. His name was Joseph."
Genesis 41: 1-45

Creation (page 149)
"... and everything would be a symphony of peace if the hand that wrote all this had stopped on the fifth day of creation."
"But there was a sixth day," the sun went on.
Genesis 1: 1-31

Treasure (page 159)
Where your treasure is, there also will be your heart," the alchemist had told him.
Matthew 6: 19-24

Urim and Thummim (page 30)
"Take these," said the old man, holding out a white stone and a black stone that had been embedded at the center of the breastplate. "They are called Urim and Thummim. The black signifies 'yes,' and the white 'no.' When you are unable to read the omens, they will help you to do so. Always ask an objective question."
Exodus 28: 30
Numbers 27: 21
Deuteronomy 33: 8
Ezra 2: 63

Each group must do the following:
1. Summarize the Biblical reference
2. Read the correlating pages from *The Alchemist*
3. Explain the connection between the two and how the allusion is effective in comprehending the novel
4. Illustrate the connection between the two, using captions from both works

Activity #5
Call on each group to share its findings. Students should listen and take notes.

LESSON TEN

Objectives
To review all of the vocabulary work done in this unit

Activity
Choose one (or more) of the vocabulary review activities listed below and spend your class period as directed in the activity. Some of the materials for these review activities are located in the Vocabulary Resource Materials section in this LitPlan.

VOCABULARY REVIEW ACTIVITIES

1. Divide your class into two teams and have an old-fashioned spelling or definition bee.

2. Give each of your students (or students in groups of two, three, or four) a *The Alchemist* Vocabulary Word Search Puzzle. The person (group) to find all of the vocabulary words in the puzzle first wins.

3. Give students a *The Alchemist* Vocabulary Word Search Puzzle without the word list. The person or group to find the most vocabulary words in the puzzle wins.

4. Use a *The Alchemist* Vocabulary Crossword Puzzle. Put the puzzle onto a transparency on the overhead projector (so everyone can see it), and do the puzzle together as a class.

5. Give students a *The Alchemist* Vocabulary Matching Worksheet to do.

6. Divide your class into two teams. Use *The Alchemist* vocabulary words with their letters jumbled as a word list. Student 1 from Team A faces off against Student 1 from Team B. Write the first jumbled word on the board. The first student (1A or 1B) to unscramble the word wins the chance for his/her team to score points. If 1A wins the jumble, go to student 2A and give him/her a definition. He/she must give you the correct spelling of the vocabulary word which fits that definition. If he/she does, Team A scores a point, and you give student 3A a definition for which you expect a correctly spelled matching vocabulary word. Continue giving Team A definitions until some team member makes an incorrect response. An incorrect response sends the game back to the jumbled-word face off, this time with students 2A and 2B. Instead of repeating giving definitions to the first few students of each team, continue with the student after the one who gave the last incorrect response on the team. For example, if Team B wins the jumbled-word face-off, and student 5B gave the last incorrect answer for Team B, you would start this round of definition questions with student 6B, and so on. The team with the most points wins!

7. Have students write a story in which they correctly use as many vocabulary words as possible. Have students read their compositions orally. Post the most original compositions on your bulletin board.

8. Play *I Have, Who Has?* *NOTE: This requires preparation in advance. On 3x5 cards, write a vocabulary word on one side and a definition to another word on the other side of the card. Once you have completed a set, pass the cards out randomly, keeping one for yourself. You will start the game by saying, "Who has..." and reading the definition on the card. The student who has the word on his/her card that matches the definition shouts, "I Have..." and reads the word. He/she then turns over the card and says "Who has..." and play continues until all the words/cards have been gone through.

9. Divide the class into two teams and play Baseball. The "pitcher" reads the definition of a word and in order to get a "hit" the "batter" must give the correct word to match the definition. For this game, though, only one strike is allowed! If the "batter" gives the correct word, he/she moves to the first base and the next "batter" comes up for another word. Score is kept like baseball with three outs and the teams switch places.

LESSON ELEVEN

<u>Objectives</u>
1. To demonstrate co-operative learning skills through working in groups
2. To demonstrate comprehension of the use of descriptive language
3. To develop critical thinking skills through the analysis of works of art
4. To relate ideas inspired by works of art to *The Alchemist*

<u>Activity #1</u>
Divide the class into groups of three or four and have each student fold two sheets of paper into quadrants (fold once horizontally and then once vertically). For each side of the papers, you will have four quadrants that should then be labeled: Characterization, Setting, Symbolism, and Situation (Conflict). The students will end up with four sets, one for each of the paintings listed below.

Project an image of one of the following paintings onto a wall or screen. Suggested works:
A Desert Encampment by Gustave Achille Guillaumet (French, 1840-1887)
A Mediterranean Courtyard by Jean-Francois Raffaelli (French, 1850-1924)
The Return (Hagar and Ishmael) by Gustave Boulanger (French, 1824-1888)
Echo and Narcissus by John William Waterhouse (English, 1849-1917)

These works are easily accessible on the Internet by using a search engine for each title.

Each student, after conferring with members of his/her group, will fill in one of the quadrant sets with details as follows:

Characterization: Look closely at the people in the painting. List at least three possible character traits they might possess based on your examination. Also, use strong adjectives to write a description of each person in the painting.

Setting: Based on the background of the painting, give at least four adjective-adjective-noun combinations that describe the setting (such as "big blue house").

Symbolism: Examine at least four objects in the painting and suggest why the artist decided to include them. What might they symbolize?

Situation (Conflict): What story is the painting telling? What is going on? How does the character relate to the setting? What do the objects have to do with the character or the setting?

<u>Activity #2</u>
Repeat the above activity with the remaining three paintings until each student has four completed sets (on the backs and fronts of both pieces of folded paper).

<u>Activity #3</u>
Each student must select one of the paintings and its corresponding set of notes, and write a paragraph linking the painting to the novel *The Alchemist*. The paragraph might be a deleted scene that the student is re-creating, or it might be an additional dialogue between characters that was edited out of the novel. Allow students to be creative, as long as the paragraph can justifiably relate to the novel.

Activity #4
(For Homework):

Choose the questions from the Extra Discussion Questions/Writing Assignments which seem most appropriate for your students. A class discussion of these questions is most effective if students have been given the opportunity to formulate answers to the questions prior to the discussion. To this end, you may either have all the students formulate answers to all the questions, divide your class into groups and assign one or more questions to each group, or you could assign one question to each student in your class. The option you choose will make a difference in the amount of class time needed for this activity. the class discussion of these questions is scheduled for Lesson Fourteen.

NOTE: The use of graphic organizers may be helpful to students in preparing their answers. Encourage them to use any diagrams or graphics that they feel are necessary.

EXTRA DISCUSSION QUESTIONS *The Alchemist*

Interpretive

1. Discuss three positive and three negative character traits for Santiago. What do these traits show you about the kind of person the boy is?
2. Discuss at least three specific character traits for each of the following: the gypsy woman, the king, the crystal merchant, the thief, the Englishman, Fatima, and the alchemist. What do each of these traits say about their characters?
3. What seems to be the main conflict in Paulo Coelho's *The Alchemist*? Fully describe the conflict and how it is (or is not) resolved.
4. How does the fact that the novel is set in both Spain and Africa play an important part in the events of the plot? What elements of life in these countries seem to play a key role in the main conflict? How does the setting differ from your own culture?
5. What elements of the setting are important to this novel? How would the novel been different if it had been set in the Australian Outback? America's Wild west?
6. Examine each of the boy's "teachers" throughout his journey. What lesson does he learn from each?
7. Describe the climax of the novel. How does the boy react to the climax?

Critical

8. Explain how Langston Hughes's poem "A Dream Deferred" relates to *The Alchemist*. What are both authors suggesting about dreams?
9. Explain the connection between the myth of Narcissus and *The Alchemist*. Why do you suppose Paulo Coelho selected this myth as a prologue to his tale?
10. Explain the five obligations from the Koran that are expected of every Muslim. What do these obligations show about the culture of the people? How does the crystal merchant honor his obligations?
11. Explain the role the king of Salem plays in the boy's adventure. What does he represent to Santiago? What about the crystal merchant's role? Fatima's? The Alchemist's?
12. The old man tells the boy that he is the King of Salem. One possibility is that he is the King of Jerusalem. What might be the significance of this? Suppose that the reference is to Salem, Massachusetts. How might the connotation of this city change the significance to the novel? Explain how this could be a source of irony.
13. Explain the following Biblical allusions: Joseph of Egypt, The Roman Centurion, Creation, The Treasure of the Heart, Urim and Thummim.
14. Explain the symbolism of the boy's dream.
15. How is it fitting that the boy should come to work for a crystal merchant? What might the crystal symbolize for the boy? What might it symbolize for the merchant?
16. How is the meeting with the refugee at the Pyramids a source of irony? How does the boy's original dream play a role in the irony?
17. Santiago is reunited with Fatima at the end of the novel. What does waiting show about her character?
18. Explain the main theme of this novel. What is Paulo Coelho's message to his readers?

Critical/Personal Response

19. What do you suppose might be the source of Santiago's discontent in the seminary that eventually leads him to become a shepherd? What does he hope to learn? What is significant about the boy's choice of occupation?

20. Compare Santiago's response to the dream in Spain with that of the marauder at the Pyramids. How might the story have been different if Santiago had responded as the marauder?
21. Suppose that Santiago had decided to have Fatima accompany him on his journey instead of leaving her to wait for his return. How might the story been different?
22. Suppose Santiago decided to stay with the crystal merchant instead of pursuing his Personal Legend. What aspects of the plot would have been changed?

Personal Response

23. Did you enjoy this novel? Why or why not?
24. What age do you think is most appropriate for reading novels like *The Alchemist*? Why might age make a difference with this type of novel?
25. Did you feel challenged when reading this novel? What types of challenges may have come forward for you?
26. Do you intend to read more books of this type? Why or why not?
27. Which of the characters do you identify with the most? Why?

LESSON TWELVE

<u>Objectives</u>
1. To practice writing skills through planning and polishing character journals
2. To practice independent work skills

<u>Activity #1</u>
Tell students to organize their journal entries and create booklets that might be believable for each character. Perhaps your Art department could provide some supplies (construction paper, colored pencils, ribbon, etc.) that students could use.

<u>Activity #2</u>
If students finish before the class time is over, they may work on their independent reading projects.

LESSON THIRTEEN

Objectives
1. To demonstrate peer response skills through sharing character journals
2. To practice oral reading skills through reading aloud character journal entries

Activity #1
Pair students up and allow them to trade character journals for critical response. Using the following Peer Response sheet, each should read the journals and respond accordingly (use the lines marked Editor).

When finished, return journals and peer response sheet to the writer. Each student is to add his reactions to the responses on the Peer Response sheet. Use the lines marked Writer.

Activity #2
Have students share character journal entries orally. (They might even use character voices when appropriate!)

Editor's Name _____   Date _____

Writer's Name _____   Assignment _____

Peer Editing for Writing Assignments

A. Was the character's voice clearly "heard"?

If your answer is "yes," be sure to tell the writer what he/she did that you especially liked. If your answer is "no," tell the writer what he/she could have included in order to write a better journal entry.

Editor: _____
_____

Writer: _____
_____

B. Did he/she provide enough details to support his/her journal entry topics?

If your answer is "yes," be sure to tell the writer what you especially liked about his/her response. If your answer is "no," you must tell the writer how he/she could improve his/her response (adding specific details that were missed, connecting to topic better).

Editor: _____
_____

Writer: _____
_____

C. Identify sentence type

Be sure to know the difference between simple, simple with compound subject, simple with compound predicate, compound, complex, and compound-complex. Using only one journal entry, correctly identify the first eight sentence types. If there is sufficient sentence structure variety, tell the writer what he/she did well. If not, explain what he/she could have done differently.

Sentence 1: _____

Sentence 5: _____

Sentence 2: _____

Sentence 6: _____

Sentence 3: _____

Sentence 7: _____

Sentence 4: _____

Sentence 8: _____

Editor: _____
_____

Writer: _____
_____

Alchemist Peer Editing Page 2

D. Address the Focus Correction Areas

Did the writer follow the specifics of the journal entries such as (address each individually):

Organization:
Editor: _____

Writer: _____

Use of vocabulary words as directed:
Editor: _____

Writer: _____

Correct relevance to the text:
Editor: _____

Writer: _____

E. Check for errors in grammar, spelling, punctuation, etc.

Editor: _____

Writer: _____

LESSON FOURTEEN

Objectives
1. To demonstrate an understanding of the novel beyond the factual questions asked in the study guide
2. To practice public speaking skills through sharing answers to discussion questions

Activity

Students will share responses to the Extra Discussion Questions assigned during Lesson Eleven. All students should take notes during the discussion.

LESSON FIFTEEN

<u>Objectives</u>
1. To demonstrate writing skills through the completion of an in-class writing assignment
2. To demonstrate the ability to work independently

<u>Activity</u>
Distribute Writing Assignment #3 to each student and discuss the directions in detail. Give students the remaining time to write the essay in class.

WRITING ASSIGNMENT #3 *The Alchemist*

PROMPT
You will read two quotations and select one you feel best supports the main idea of Paulo Coelho's *The Alchemist*. In your essay, you need to indicate whether or not you agree with the main idea of the quotation and then defend your position by using specific textual support from *The Alchemist*.

PREWRITING
Choose one of the following:

"What a man thinks of himself, that is which determines, or rather indicates, his fate."
Henry David Thoreau

"There are some people who live in a dream world, and there are some who face reality; and then there are those who turn one into the other."
Douglas Evertt

Decide whether or not you agree with the main idea of your selected quotation and choose specific textual evidence from *The Alchemist* that best supports your position.

DRAFTING
In your introduction, explain the meaning of the selected quotation and state whether or not you agree with the speaker (without using first person). This is best done by indicating whether or not the statement is true. At the end of your introduction, create a thesis statement in which you refer to Paulo Coelho's novel as support for your position. Your body paragraphs should contain at least two specific scenes from *The Alchemist* (complete with embedded quotations and parenthetical citations) that support your position on the quotation. Conclude your essay with some sort of a challenge to your reader with reference to the quotation.

PROMPT
When you finish the rough draft of your paper, ask a student who sits near you to read it. After reading your rough draft, he/she should tell you what he/she liked best about your work, which parts were difficult to understand, and ways in which your work could be improved. Reread your paper considering your critic's comments, and make the corrections you think are necessary.

PROOFREADING
Do a final proofreading of your paper double-checking your grammar, spelling, organization, and the clarity of your ideas.

LESSONS SIXTEEN AND SEVENTEEN

Objectives
1. To follow-up with Writing Assignment #1
2. To practice public speaking skills through delivering a presentation
3. To practice listening skills through listening to peer presentations

Activity #1
Poll the class for information students learned about the legends of the Philosopher's Stone and the Elixir of Life through their research. Each student should have something to contribute to the discussion.

Activity #2
Each student will share a 7-10 minute presentation about the companion piece he/she selected for Writing Assignment #1. Each should include the following:

1. A brief synopsis of the work

2. Character sketches for both the protagonist and the antagonist discussing character traits

3. How the legends of the Philosopher's Stone and/or the Elixir of Life relate to the work

4. How the work relates to *The Alchemist*

Presentation Evaluation Sheet

Name _____

Title: _____

Author: _____

Each of the following will be graded on a scale of 1-5, with 1 being the lowest; each is worth 20% of the overall grade.

> **Part I:** Student provided accurate information about the Philosopher's Stone and the Elixir of Life.
> **Part II:** Student provided brief and accurate summary of the independent work
> **Part III:** Student provided accurate character sketches for both the antagonist and the protagonist in the independent work
> **Part IV:** Student relates how the Philosopher's Stone and/or the Elixir of Life play a role in the independent work
> **Part V:** Student connects the independent work to *The Alchemist*

Part I: _____

Part II: _____

Part III: _____

Part IV: _____

Part V: _____

Total: _____   X Five   Total Grade: _____

Comments:

LESSON EIGHTEEN

Objectives
1. To review all the material covered in the unit
2. To help students prepare for the unit test

Activity
Choose one or more of the activities listed below and use your class time as directed.

REVIEW GAMES AND ACTIVITIES

1. Ask the class to make up a unit test for *The Alchemist*. The test should have 4 sections: matching, true/false, short answer, and essay. Students may use 1/2 of the class period to make the test and then swap papers and use the other 1/2 of the period to take a test a classmate has devised (open book). You may want to use the unit test included in this packet or take questions from the students' unit tests to formulate your own test.

2. Take 1/2 period for students to make up true and false questions (including the answers). Collect the papers and divide the class into two teams. Draw a big Tic-Tac-Toe board on the chalk board. Make one team X and one team O. Ask questions to each side, giving each student one turn. If the question is answered correctly, that student's team's letter (X or O) is placed in the box. If the answer is incorrect, no letter is placed in the box. The object is to get three in a row like Tic-Tac-Toe. You may want to keep track of the number of games won for each team.

3. Take 1/2 period for students to make up questions (true/false and short answer). Collect the questions. Divide the class into two teams. You'll alternate asking questions to individual members of teams A and B (like in a spelling bee). The question keeps going from A to B until it is correctly answered, then a new question is asked. A correct answer does not allow the team to get another question. Correct answers are +2 points; incorrect answers are -1 point.

4. Have students pair up and quiz each other from their study guides and class notes.

5. Give students a *The Alchemist* crossword puzzle to complete.

6. Divide your class into two teams. Use *The Alchemist* crossword words with their letters jumbled as a word list. Student 1 from Team A faces off against Student 1 from Team B. You write the first jumbled word on the board. The first student (1A or 1B) to unscramble the word wins the chance for his/her team to score points. If 1A wins the jumble, go to student 2A and give him/her a clue. He/she must give you the correct word which matches that clue. If he/she does, Team A scores a point, and you give student 3A a clue for which you expect another correct response. An incorrect response sends the game back to the jumbled-word face off, this time with students 2A and 2B. Instead of repeating giving clues to the first few students of each team, continue with the student after the one who gave the last incorrect response on the team. For example, if Team B wins the jumbled-word face-off, and student 5B gave the last incorrect answer for Team B, you would start this round of clue questions with student 6B and so on. The team with the most points wins!

7. Play *What's My Line?*. This is similar to the old television show. Students assume the roles of different characters from the novel. One student gives clues to the class, or to a panel of contestants. The contestants try to guess the identity of the guest. Students may enjoy assisting you in creating rules and procedures for the game.

8. Play *Jeopardy*. Divide the class into two groups. Assign each group a category or chapter

from the novel and have them devise answers for that category. Play the game according to the television show procedures.

9. Play *Drawing on the Details*. This is similar to *Pictionary*. Divide students into teams. A student from one team draws a scene from the novel. (You may want to specify the book or section.) Drawings should be kept simple, to keep the pace lively. Students in the opposing team locate the scene in their books and read it aloud. If they are incorrect, the illustrator's team has a chance to guess. Involve students in setting up a scoring system and any other necessary rules.

10. Play *I Have, Who Has?*. *NOTE This requires preparation in advance. On 3x5 cards, write a clue word on one side and a clue/definition question to another clue word on the other side of the card. Once you have completed a set, pass the cards out randomly, keeping one for yourself. You will start the game by saying, "Who has..." and reading the definition/question on the card. The student who has the answer on his/her card that matches the definition/question shouts, "I have..." and reads the answer. He/she then turns over the card and says, "Who has..." and play continues until all the cards have been gone through.

11. Divide the class into two teams and play *Baseball*. The "pitcher" reads a question about the novel and in order to get a "hit" the "batter" must correctly answer the question. For this game, though, only one strike is allowed! If the "batter" gives the correct answer, he/she moves to the first base and the next "batter" comes up for another question. Score is kept like baseball with three outs and the teams switch places.

LESSON NINETEEN

Objectives
To test the students' understanding of the main ideas and themes in *The Alchemist*

Activity #1
Distribute the unit tests. Go over the instructions in detail and allow the students the entire class period to complete the exam.

NOTES ABOUT THE UNIT TESTS IN THIS UNIT:

There are 5 different unit tests included in the LitPlan Teacher Pack. Two are short answer, two are multiple choice. There is one advanced short answer test. The answers to the advanced short answer test will be based on the discussions you have had during class and should be graded accordingly. You should choose the tests and/or test parts which best suit your needs. Matching and short answer tests have answer keys. For essay type questions, grade according to your own criteria based on class discussions and the level of your students. Also, you will need to choose vocabulary words to read orally for the vocabulary section of the short answer tests.

Activity #2
Collect all test papers and assigned books prior to the end of the class period.

UNIT TESTS

The Alchemist SHORT ANSWER UNIT TEST 1

I. Matching/Identify

____ 1.	SANTIAGO	A.	Occupation chosen by the boy
____ 2.	PRIEST	B.	Country where the boy's journey begins
____ 3.	SHEPHERD	C.	Boy who saved Egypt through dream interpretation
____ 4.	DREAM	D.	The boy
____ 5.	GYPSY	E.	Tells the boy to show him where there is life in the desert
____ 6.	SALEM	F.	Hooded men of the desert who provide information
____ 7.	CANDY	G.	The principle of favorability; beginner's ___
____ 8.	CRYSTAL	H.	Sight of the distracted boy in the marketplace
____ 9.	FATIMA	I.	Befriends the boy in the caravan
____ 10.	ENGLISHMAN	J.	Continent over which the boy travels
____ 11.	NARCISSUS	K.	Boy's destination based on his dream
____ 12.	LUCK	L.	Tells the boy what his dream means
____ 13.	SWORD	M.	Merchant's unvisited Pilgrimage destination
____ 14.	BEDOUINS	N.	Helps the boy in the market place after he is robbed; ___ seller
____ 15.	JOSEPH	O.	This leads the boy to begin his journey
____ 16.	ALCHEMIST	P.	For whom the lake weeps
____ 17.	PYRAMIDS	Q.	Occupation the boy's parents chose for him
____ 18.	AFRICA	R.	She waits for the boy's return.
____ 19.	SPAIN	S.	The old man who knew all about the boy; King of ___
____ 20.	MECCA	T.	The boy's help greatly increases his business; ___ Merchant

II. Short Answer

1. Why does the lake weep for Narcissus?

2. Why does the shepherd decide to see the Gypsy woman?

3. According to the old man, what is the world's greatest lie?

4. What is the "principle of favorability" that the old man speaks of?

5. According to the "wisest of wise men," what is the secret of happiness?

6. In order to attract more business after working there for one month, what does the boy suggest that the crystal merchant allow him to do?

7. Why does the merchant claim to feel worse than he did before the boy arrived to work for him?

8. How did the camel driver who befriended the boy come to be in this line of work?

9. What is the "Emerald Tablet"?

10. What "omens from the desert" does the boy share with the chieftains of the oasis?

11. When riding out into the desert, what does the alchemist instruct the boy to show him?

12. Why is the boy disappointed when the alchemist writes in the sand what is inscribed on the Emerald Tablet?

13. What do the armed tribesmen find in the alchemist's bag?

14. What does the desert ask the boy to explain to it?

15. What is the chief's plan for the two men who wanted to end the bet with the boy?

16. According to the boy, why does alchemy exist?

17. Describe the dream the alchemist tells to the boy.

18. What warning does the boy's heart whisper as he is about to climb a large dune?

19. What piece of advice does the leader of the refugees give the boy before he leaves?

20. What does the boy find beneath the sycamore tree in the ruined church?

III. Essay
1. Discuss the meaning of the following quotation and then relate to three specific choices that the boy made in *The Alchemist* that had a profound effect on his destiny.
"Destiny is no matter of chance. It is a matter of choice. It is not a thing to be waited for; it is a thing to be achieved."
William Jennings Bryan

IV. Vocabulary
	A. Write the vocabulary words you are given. After writing them down, go back and write in their definitions.

Word	Definition
1	
2	
3	
4	
5	
6	
7	
8	
9	
10	

The Alchemist SHORT ANSWER UNIT TEST 1 Answer Key

I. Matching/Identify

D	1.	SANTIAGO	A.	Occupation chosen by the boy
Q	2.	PRIEST	B.	Country where the boy's journey begins
A	3.	SHEPHERD	C.	Boy who saved Egypt through dream interpretation
O	4.	DREAM	D.	The boy
L	5.	GYPSY	E.	Tells the boy to show him where there is life in the desert
S	6.	SALEM	F.	Hooded men of the desert who provide information
N	7.	CANDY	G.	The principle of favorability; beginner's ___
T	8.	CRYSTAL	H.	Sight of the distracted boy in the marketplace
R	9.	FATIMA	I.	Befriends the boy in the caravan
I	10.	ENGLISHMAN	J.	Continent over which the boy travels
P	11.	NARCISSUS	K.	Boy's destination based on his dream
G	12.	LUCK	L.	Tells the boy what his dream means
H	13.	SWORD	M.	Merchant's unvisited Pilgrimage destination
F	14.	BEDOUINS	N.	Helps the boy in the market place after he is robbed; ___ seller
C	15.	JOSEPH	O.	This leads the boy to begin his journey
E	16.	ALCHEMIST	P.	For whom the lake weeps
K	17.	PYRAMIDS	Q.	Occupation the boy's parents chose for him
J	18.	AFRICA	R.	She waits for the boy's return.
B	19.	SPAIN	S.	The old man who knew all about the boy; King of ___
M	20.	MECCA	T.	The boy's help greatly increases his business; ___ Merchant

II. Short Answer

1. Why does the lake weep for Narcissus?
   It weeps because each time Narcissus knelt beside the lake's banks, the lake's only beauty was reflected in Narcissus's eyes.

2. Why does the shepherd decide to see the Gypsy woman?
   He wants the Gypsy woman to interpret a recurring dream.

3. According to the old man, what is the world's greatest lie?
   He says that the world's greatest lie is that "at a certain point in our lives, we lose control of what's happening to us, and our lives become controlled by fate."

4. What is the "principle of favorability" that the old man speaks of?
   The old man says that it is the beginner's luck because "there is a force that wants you to realize your Personal Legend; it whets your appetite with a taste of success."

5. According to the "wisest of wise men," what is the secret of happiness?
   The wisest of the wise men says that the secret of happiness is "to see all the marvels of the world, and never to forget the drops of oil on the spoon."

6. In order to attract more business after working there for one month, what does the boy suggest that the crystal merchant allow him to do?
   The boy wants to build a display case to place outside the store to attract more customers. In this way, the boy can sell more crystal and earn more money to buy sheep.

7. Why does the merchant claim to feel worse than he did before the boy arrived to work for him?
   The boy has shown the merchant possibilities he's never dreamed of, but the man does not like change. The merchant now knows of things he should be able to accomplish, but he simply does not want to do them.

8. How did the camel driver who befriended the boy come to be in this line of work?
   The man used to own an olive orchard, but when the Nile flooded the land and ruined his orchard, he was forced into another line of work.

9. What is the "Emerald Tablet"?
   It is an emerald upon which the most important text in the literature of alchemy, containing only a few lines, had been inscribed.

10. What "omens from the desert" does the boy share with the chieftains of the oasis?
    The boy has seen a vision of men with swords attacking the oasis, so he decides to warn the chieftains of a possible onslaught.

11. When riding out into the desert, what does the alchemist instruct the boy to show him?
    The alchemist tells the boy to show him "where there is life in the desert." The boy follows the intuitions of his horse that stops by some rocks in the desert. When the alchemist puts his hand in a hole near the rocks, he pulls out a cobra.

12. Why is the boy disappointed when the alchemist writes in the sand what is inscribed on the Emerald Tablet?
    It is written in a code he does not understand, so it makes no more sense to him than the Englishman's books.

13. What do the armed tribesmen find in the alchemist's bag?
    They find a small flask filled with liquid and a yellow glass egg that is slightly larger than a chicken egg.

14. What does the desert ask the boy to explain to it?
    The desert wants to know what love is.

15. What is the chief's plan for the two men who wanted to end the bet with the boy?
    The chief plans to remove them from their positions because "true men of the desert are not afraid."

16. According to the boy, why does alchemy exist?
    Alchemy exists so that "everyone will search for his treasure, find it, and then want to be better than he was in his former life."

17. Describe the dream the alchemist tells to the boy.
    A man in Ancient Rome had two sons: a soldier and a poet. An angel told the man in a dream that one of his sons' words would be remembered throughout time. When the man died, he asked the angel to tell him what words his son the poet had written that were so profound. The angel replied that it was the soldier's words to a Jewish rabbi that were remembered.

18. What warning does the boy's heart whisper as he is about to climb a large dune?
    "Be aware of the place where you are brought to tears. That's where I am and that is where your treasure is."

19. What piece of advice does the leader of the refugees give the boy before he leaves?
    He tells the boy not to believe in dreams because he once, on the very spot where they now stood, had a dream that he was in an old church in Spain, and he found gold beneath a sycamore tree growing in the ruins of the sacristy. He said that he was not so stupid as to cross the desert because of a dream.

20. What does the boy find beneath the sycamore tree in the ruined church?
    He finds a conquistador's treasure that had been buried there. The boy gives 10% to the gypsy woman who had interpreted his dream, and he uses the rest to go back to Fatima.

IV. Vocabulary

   Write the vocabulary words and definitions you will use for this test.

Word	Definition
1	
2	
3	
4	
5	
6	
7	
8	
9	
10	

The Alchemist SHORT ANSWER UNIT TEST 2

I. Matching/Identify

____ 1. SANTIAGO   A. For whom the lake weeps
____ 2. PRIEST   B. Hooded men of the desert who provide information
____ 3. SHEPHERD   C. The principle of favorability; beginner's ___
____ 4. DREAM   D. The boy's help greatly increases his business; ___ Merchant
____ 5. GYPSY   E. This leads the boy to begin his journey
____ 6. SALEM   F. Befriends the boy in the caravan
____ 7. CANDY   G. Continent over which the boy travels
____ 8. CRYSTAL   H. Tells the boy to show him where there is life in the desert
____ 9. FATIMA   I. The old man who knew all about the boy; King of ___
____ 10. ENGLISHMAN   J. The boy
____ 11. NARCISSUS   K. Sight of the distracted boy in the marketplace
____ 12. LUCK   L. She waits for the boy's return.
____ 13. SWORD   M. Boy's destination based on his dream
____ 14. BEDOUINS   N. Helps the boy in the market place after he is robbed; ___ seller
____ 15. JOSEPH   O. Tells the boy what his dream means
____ 16. ALCHEMIST   P. Boy who saved Egypt through dream interpretation
____ 17. PYRAMIDS   Q. Merchant's unvisited Pilgrimage destination
____ 18. AFRICA   R. Country where the boy's journey begins
____ 19. SPAIN   S. Occupation chosen by the boy
____ 20. MECCA   T. Occupation the boy's parents chose for him

II. Short Answer

1. How does the boy spend his time when the merchant tells him he cannot shear his sheep until the afternoon?

2. Describe the shepherd boy's recurring dream.

3. According to the old man, what is the one great truth on this planet?

4. What are Urim and Thummim?

5. After helping the candy seller erect his stall in the plaza, to what realization did the shepherd boy come?

6. Why didn't the crystal merchant ever go on a pilgrimage to Mecca?

7. When the boy tells the merchant that he is going to be leaving to return to his country to buy sheep, he asks for the merchant's blessing. What does the merchant say about the boy's journey home?

8. What news does the caravan leader learn that causes the members to become more cautious while traveling, especially at night?

9. Who is Fatima?

10. What decision does the head chieftain make about the boy's visions?

11. What words does the alchemist say that echo those of the old king?

12. What does the desert come to mean for Fatima?

13. According to the alchemist, what is worse than suffering?

14. Why don't the tribesmen take what is in the alchemist's bag?

15. When asked who taught the boy the language of the desert and wind, what is the boy's reply?

16. How does the sun claim to know about love?

17. What feat does the alchemist perform at the monastery?

18. What did the centurion say that was remembered for all time?

19. As the boy wept at the sight that beheld him, what does he notice in the sand?

20. How does the boy finance his journey back to Spain?

III. Composition
1. Explain the meaning of the following quotation, and discuss two characters from *The Alchemist* who relate to Campbell's words--one who did as Campbell suggests, and one who didn't.
   "We must be willing to get rid of the life we've planned, so as to have the life that is waiting for us. The old skin has to be shed before the new one can come."
   Joseph Campbell

IV. Vocabulary
> A. Write the vocabulary words you are given. After writing them down, go back and write in their definitions.

Word	Definition
1	
2	
3	
4	
5	
6	
7	
8	
9	
10	

The Alchemist SHORT ANSWER UNIT TEST 2 Answer Key

I. Matching/Identify

J	1.	SANTIAGO	A.	For whom the lake weeps
T	2.	PRIEST	B.	Hooded men of the desert who provide information
S	3.	SHEPHERD	C.	The principle of favorability; beginner's ___
E	4.	DREAM	D.	The boy's help greatly increases his business; ___ Merchant
O	5.	GYPSY	E.	This leads the boy to begin his journey
I	6.	SALEM	F.	Befriends the boy in the caravan
N	7.	CANDY	G.	Continent over which the boy travels
D	8.	CRYSTAL	H.	Tells the boy to show him where there is life in the desert
L	9.	FATIMA	I.	The old man who knew all about the boy; King of ___
F	10.	ENGLISHMAN	J.	The boy
A	11.	NARCISSUS	K.	Sight of the distracted boy in the marketplace
C	12.	LUCK	L.	She waits for the boy's return.
K	13.	SWORD	M.	Boy's destination based on his dream
B	14.	BEDOUINS	N.	Helps the boy in the market place after he is robbed; ___ seller
P	15.	JOSEPH	O.	Tells the boy what his dream means
H	16.	ALCHEMIST	P.	Boy who saved Egypt through dream interpretation
M	17.	PYRAMIDS	Q.	Merchant's unvisited Pilgrimage destination
G	18.	AFRICA	R.	Country where the boy's journey begins
R	19.	SPAIN	S.	Occupation chosen by the boy
Q	20.	MECCA	T.	Occupation the boy's parents chose for him

II. Short Answer
1. How does the boy spend his time when the merchant tells him he cannot shear his sheep until the afternoon?
   He talks with the merchant's daughter and becomes so engrossed in talking with her that he found himself wishing the day would never end and that the merchant would keep him waiting for three days.

2. Describe the shepherd boy's recurring dream.
   He has twice dreamt that a child came and played with his sheep. Suddenly, the child grabbed the hands of the shepherd and they were transported to the Egyptian Pyramids. The child told the shepherd that if he went there to the Pyramids, he would find a great treasure. However just as he was asking the child the location of the treasure, the shepherd woke up.

3. According to the old man, what is the one great truth on this planet?
   The one great truth is that "whoever you are, or whatever it is that you do, when you really want something, it's because that desire is originated in the soul of the universe. It's your mission on earth."

4. What are Urim and Thummim?
   They are two stones taken from the golden breastplate of the old man that can be used for divination. When asked an objective question, Urim is a black stone that signifies "yes" and Thummim is a white stone that signifies "no."

5. After helping the candy seller erect his stall in the plaza, to what realization did the shepherd boy come?
   He realizes that although the candy seller spoke Arabic and he spoke Spanish, the two had been able to understand one another perfectly. He concludes that there must be a language that does not depend on words.

6. Why didn't the crystal merchant ever go on a pilgrimage to Mecca?
   He intended to do it when he earned enough money. Once the business got going, he felt he couldn't leave the shop in someone else's hands long enough to go to Mecca.

7. When the boy tells the merchant that he is going to be leaving to return to his country to buy sheep, he asks for the merchant's blessing. What does the merchant say about the boy's journey home?
   The merchant says that just as he knows that he will never go to Mecca, the boy will not be returning home to buy his sheep.

8. What news does the caravan leader learn that causes the members to become more cautious while traveling, especially at night?
   He learns that there are tribal wars taking place in the desert, and the caravan begins to travel in silence and keep its fires lower so as not to draw attention to themselves.

9. Who is Fatima?
   Fatima is a young woman who lives at the oasis. At first glance when they meet at a well, the boy falls in love with her. At every opportunity, the boy tries to meet Fatima at the well so that he can talk to her.

10. What decision does the head chieftain make about the boy's visions?
    The chieftain decides that he will heed the warnings and arm his people the next day, although it is against tradition to carry weapons in an oasis. For every ten enemies killed by the weapons, the boy will receive one piece of gold. If no enemies attack, in order to keep the weapons from refusing to work when needed in the future, one of the weapons will be used on the boy.

11. What words does the alchemist say that echo those of the old king?
    "When a person really desires something, all the universe conspires to help that person to realize his dream."

12. What does the desert come to mean for Fatima?
    The desert now represents the hope for the boy's return.
13. According to the alchemist, what is worse than suffering?
    The alchemist tells the boy that the fear of suffering is worse than the suffering itself.
14. Why don't the tribesmen take what is in the alchemist's bag?
    When the alchemist tells them that the liquid is the Elixir of Life and that the glass egg is the Philosopher's Stone, they merely laugh and do not believe him.
15. When asked who taught the boy the language of the desert and wind, what is the boy's reply?
    The boy states that his heart taught him the language.
16. How does the sun claim to know about love?
    The sun tells the boy that it knows about love because it is aware that if it came even a little bit closer to the earth, everything would die, and the Soul of the World would no longer exist. Because the sun and the Soul of the World work together to cause the plants to grow and the sheep to survive, the sun gives the world warmth, and the Soul of the World gives the sun a reason to exist.
17. What feat does the alchemist perform at the monastery?
    The alchemist turns lead into gold. He breaks it into four pieces: one for the monk for his generosity, one for the boy to make up for what the alchemist had taken from him to give the general, one for himself, and one for the monk to hold for the boy if he were to ever need it.
18. What did the centurion say that was remembered for all time?
    "My Lord, I am not worthy that you should come under my roof. But only speak a word and my servant will be healed."
19. As the boy wept at the sight that beheld him, what does he notice in the sand?
    He notices that where his tears fell in the sand, a sacred scarab beetle came scuttling up. He believes it is an omen.
20. How does the boy finance his journey back to Spain?
    He goes back to the monastery where the alchemist had turned the lead into gold. The alchemist had asked the monk to hold a piece of the gold for the boy if he should ever need it. The boy claims the gold and uses it to get back to the churchyard in Spain where he once spent the night with his sheep and where he had his dream about the Pyramids.

IV. Vocabulary
   Write the vocabulary words and definitions you will use for this test.

Word	Definition
1	
2	
3	
4	
5	
6	
7	
8	
9	
10	

The Alchemist ADVANCED SHORT ANSWER UNIT TEST

I. Matching

____	1.	SANTIAGO	A. Boy who saved Egypt through dream interpretation
____	2.	PRIEST	B. Love never keeps a man from pursuing his Personal ___.
____	3.	GYPSY	C. Occupation the boy's parents chose for him
____	4.	SALEM	D. Be aware of the place where you are brought to ___.
____	5.	FATIMA	E. Sent out by the alchemist to hunt each day
____	6.	ENGLISHMAN	F. The boy
____	7.	URIM	G. When one wants to do something, it is because that desire originated in the soul of the universe; the world's greatest ___.
____	8.	ELIXIR	H. The greatest lie: Our lives become controlled by ___.
____	9.	STONE	I. Solid part of the Master Work; Philosopher's ___
____	10.	JOSEPH	J. Divination stones given to the boy; ___ and Thummim
____	11.	ALCHEMIST	K. Merchant's unvisited Pilgrimage destination
____	12.	CENTURION	L. Muslim book of faith
____	13.	MONK	M. Befriends the boy in the caravan
____	14.	FATE	N. Tells the boy what his dream means
____	15.	MECCA	O. The old man who knew all about the boy; King of ___
____	16.	LEGEND	P. Tells the boy to show him where there is life in the desert
____	17.	FALCON	Q. Liquid part of the Master Work; ___ of Life
____	18.	TEARS	R. She waits for the boy's return.
____	19.	KORAN	S. He holds gold for the boy in case he ever needs it.
____	20.	TRUTH	T. His words of faith were to be remembered for all time.

II. Short Answer
1. Discuss at least three specific character traits for each of the following: the gypsy woman, the king, the crystal merchant, the thief, the Englishman, Fatima, and the alchemist. What do each of these traits say about their characters?

2. How does the fact that the novel is set in both Spain and Africa play an important part in the events of the plot? What elements of life in these countries seem to play a key role in the main conflict? How does the setting differ from your own culture?

3. Examine each of the boy's "teachers" throughout his journey. What lesson does he learn from each?

4. Explain the connection between the myth of Narcissus and *The Alchemist*. Why do you suppose Paulo Coelho selected this myth as a prologue to his tale?

5. Explain the following Biblical allusions: Joseph of Egypt, The Roman Centurion, Creation, The Treasure of the Heart, Urim and Thummim.

6. Explain the symbolism of the boy's dream.

7. How is it fitting that the boy should come to work for a crystal merchant? What might the crystal symbolize for the boy? What might it symbolize for the merchant?

8. How is the meeting with the refugee at the Pyramids a source of irony? How does the boy's original dream play a role in the irony?

9. Explain the main theme of this novel. What is Paulo Coelho's message to his readers?

10. What do you suppose might be the source of Santiago's discontent in the seminary that eventually leads him to become a shepherd? What does he hope to learn? What is significant about the boy's choice of occupation?

III. Composition
1. Explain how Langston Hughes's poem "A Dream Deferred" relates to *The Alchemist*. What are both authors suggesting about dreams?

IV. Vocabulary
A. Write the vocabulary words you are given. After writing them down, go back and write in their definitions.

Word	Definition
1	
2	
3	
4	
5	
6	
7	
8	
9	
10	

B. Write a paragraph about the book using 8 of the 10 vocabulary words above.

The Alchemist ADVANCED SHORT ANSWER UNIT TEST Answer Key

I. Matching

F	1.	SANTIAGO	A.	Boy who saved Egypt through dream interpretation
C	2.	PRIEST	B.	Love never keeps a man from pursuing his Personal ___.
N	3.	GYPSY	C.	Occupation the boy's parents chose for him
O	4.	SALEM	D.	Be aware of the place where you are brought to ___.
R	5.	FATIMA	E.	Sent out by the alchemist to hunt each day
M	6.	ENGLISHMAN	F.	The boy
J	7.	URIM	G.	When one wants to do something, it is because that desire originated in the soul of the universe; the world's greatest ___.
Q	8.	ELIXIR	H.	The greatest lie: Our lives become controlled by ___.
I	9.	STONE	I.	Solid part of the Master Work; Philosopher's ___
A	10.	JOSEPH	J.	Divination stones given to the boy; ___ and Thummim
P	11.	ALCHEMIST	K.	Merchant's unvisited Pilgrimage destination
T	12.	CENTURION	L.	Muslim book of faith
S	13.	MONK	M.	Befriends the boy in the caravan
H	14.	FATE	N.	Tells the boy what his dream means
K	15.	MECCA	O.	The old man who knew all about the boy; King of ___
B	16.	LEGEND	P.	Tells the boy to show him where there is life in the desert
E	17.	FALCON	Q.	Liquid part of the Master Work; ___ of Life
D	18.	TEARS	R.	She waits for the boy's return.
L	19.	KORAN	S.	He holds gold for the boy in case he ever needs it.
G	20.	TRUTH	T.	His words of faith were to be remembered for all time.

IV. Vocabulary
Write the vocabulary words and definitions you will use for this test.

Word	Definition
1	
2	
3	
4	
5	
6	
7	
8	
9	
10	

The Alchemist MULTIPLE CHOICE UNIT TEST 1

I. Matching/Identify

____ 1. SANTIAGO   A. Helps the boy in the market place after he is robbed; ___ seller
____ 2. PRIEST   B. Tells the boy what his dream means
____ 3. SHEPHERD   C. Occupation chosen by the boy
____ 4. DREAM   D. Merchant's unvisited Pilgrimage destination
____ 5. GYPSY   E. Tells the boy to show him where there is life in the desert
____ 6. SALEM   F. She waits for the boy's return.
____ 7. CANDY   G. The boy's help greatly increases his business; ___ Merchant
____ 8. CRYSTAL   H. The old man who knew all about the boy; King of ___
____ 9. FATIMA   I. The principle of favorability; beginner's ___
____ 10. ENGLISHMAN   J. Continent over which the boy travels
____ 11. NARCISSUS   K. Hooded men of the desert who provide information
____ 12. LUCK   L. Country where the boy's journey begins
____ 13. SWORD   M. For whom the lake weeps
____ 14. BEDOUINS   N. The boy
____ 15. JOSEPH   O. Befriends the boy in the caravan
____ 16. ALCHEMIST   P. Boy's destination based on his dream
____ 17. PYRAMIDS   Q. Sight of the distracted boy in the marketplace
____ 18. AFRICA   R. Occupation the boy's parents chose for him
____ 19. SPAIN   S. This leads the boy to begin his journey
____ 20. MECCA   T. Boy who saved Egypt through dream interpretation

II. Multiple Choice

1. Why does the lake weep for Narcissus?
   A. Narcissus was brutally murdered.
   B. It is grieving the loss of Narcissus.
   C. It had been able to see its own beauty in Narcissus's eyes; it wants him back.
   D. Narcissus left with a woman and it feels neglected.

2. Why does the shepherd decide to see the Gypsy woman?
   A. He wants her to tell him about his father.
   B. He wants her to tell his fortune about the merchant's daughter.
   C. He wants her to interpret a recurring dream.
   D. He wants her to make a love potion to give to the merchant's daughter.

3. According to the old man, what is the world's greatest lie?
   A. The world's greatest lie is that people have the free will to do as they wish.
   B. The world's greatest lie is that people's lives are controlled by fate.
   C. The world's greatest lie is that people cannot see into the past or the future.
   D. The world's greatest lie is that people were meant to be happy.

4. What is the "principle of favorability" that the old man speaks of?
   A. It is also known as "the survival of the fittest."
   B. It is also known as "beginner's luck."
   C. It is also known as "the will of God."
   D. It is also known as "being in the right place at the right time."

5. According to the "wisest of wise men," what is the secret of happiness?
   A. The secret of happiness is to "bloom where you are planted."
   B. The secret of happiness is to be happy for others' fortunes without bitterness.
   C. The secret is to see the world's marvels without forgetting the oil in the spoon.
   D. The secret of happiness is to be happy with what you already have.

6. In order to attract more business after working there for one month, what does the boy suggest that the crystal merchant allow him to do?
   A. He asks the merchant to let him build a display case for outside the shop.
   B. He asks the merchant to allow him to place an ad in the local papers.
   C. He asks the merchant to allow him to open a stall in the bazaar.
   D. He asks the merchant to let him paint a large billboard on the main road.

7. Why does the merchant claim to feel worse than he did before the boy arrived to work for him?
    A. The boy has helped improve business, but the merchant doesn't want the extra work.
    B. The boy has shown him how he could accomplish things, but he hates change.
    C. The merchant's daughter has fallen in love with the boy; he disapproves of it.
    D. The boy is a better seller than the crystal merchant.

8. How did the camel driver who befriended the boy come to be in this line of work?
    A. He lost his olive orchard to a flood, and he needed to care for his family.
    B. He left his position in the seminary to be able to see the world as a camel driver.
    C. He was taken as a slave as a child by a group of camel drivers; it's all he knows.
    D. He is from a family of camel drivers.

9. What is the "Emerald Tablet"?
    A. It is a jewel in the armor of the old King Salem.
    B. It is a magical stone that turns lead into gold.
    C. It is a rare jewel in the crown of the Egyptian pharaoh.
    D. It is a jewel upon which the most important text of alchemy is inscribed.

10. What "omens from the desert" does the boy share with the chieftains of the oasis?
    A. He sees two hawks fighting and then envisioned the oasis in flames.
    B. He uses Urim and Thummim and believes that the oasis is in danger.
    C. He hears the winds speak to him about the tribal wars.
    D. He sees a vision of men with swords attacking the oasis.

11. What decision does the head chieftain make about the boy's visions?
    A. He laughs that someone so young could possibly have such visions.
    B. He becomes angry and jails the boy as an enemy spy.
    C. He heeds the boy's warning, yet threatens the boy if they do not come true.
    D. He does not take the boy seriously and ignores him.

12. When riding out into the desert, what does the alchemist instruct the boy to show him?
    A. He tells the boy to show him where there is life in the desert.
    B. He tells the boy to show him the way to the Pyramids.
    C. He tells the boy to show him where he first saw the omen that led him to warn the chieftain.
    D. He tells the boy to show him how to use Urim and Thummim.

13. Why is the boy disappointed when the alchemist writes in the sand what is inscribed on the Emerald Tablet?
    A. The boy thought it would give him the secret to the Language of the World.
    B. It is written in a code the boy does not understand.
    C. The boy expected to learn how to create the Elixir of Life.
    D. The boy expected to learn how to turn any metal into gold.

14. What do the armed tribesmen find in the alchemist's bag?
    A. They find a never-ending supply of food.
    B. They find his books on alchemy.
    C. They find the boy's pouch filled with gold.
    D. They find a small flask of liquid and a yellow glass egg.

15. What does the desert ask the boy to explain to it?
    A. It wants to know how to turn lead into gold.
    B. It wants to know the Language of the World.
    C. It wants to know what love is.
    D. It wants to know the meaning of life.

16. What is the chief's plan for the two men who wanted to end the bet with the boy?
    A. He plans to replace them with the boy and the alchemist.
    B. He plans to remove them from their positions because they were afraid.
    C. He plans to execute them for their fears.
    D. He plans to reward them for not playing into the boy's hand.

17. According to the boy, why does alchemy exist?
    A. Alchemy exists to prove that man can create gold from meaningless metals.
    B. Alchemy exists in order to distinguish between those who are searching for the truth and those who are merely greedy.
    C. Alchemy exists so that everyone will search for and find his treasure, and hopefully lead a better life.
    D. Alchemy exists so that everyone can be rich.

18. Describe the dream the alchemist tells to the boy.
    A. The alchemist tells the dream of a Roman man about his two sons.
    B. The alchemist says that he had dreamed about a boy who would come to him and then turn himself into the wind.
    C. The alchemist reiterates the boy's dream from the sacristy in Spain.
    D. The alchemist says that he dreamed that he saw the boy at the Great Pyramids.

19. What warning does the boy's heart whisper as he is about to climb a large dune?
    A. His heart warns him not to climb the dune because danger lurks behind.
    B. His heart warns him to be aware of the place where he is brought to tears.
    C. His heart warns him against greed once he finds his treasure.
    D. His heart warns him not to trust anyone he meets on the other side of the dune.

20. What piece of advice does the leader of the refugees give the boy before he leaves?
    A. Never be alone in the desert after dark.
    B. Don't bother with dreams; he wasn't stupid enough to go to another country because of a dream.
    C. The boy should hurry back to the oasis before Fatima marries another.
    D. Don't tell anyone what he knows about the Language of the World.

III. Composition
1. Examine each of the boy's "teachers" throughout his journey. What lesson does he learn from each?

2. Explain the connection between the myth of Narcissus and *The Alchemist*. Why do you suppose Paulo Coelho selected this myth as a prologue to his tale?

3. How is it fitting that the boy should come to work for a crystal merchant? What might the crystal symbolize for the boy? What might it symbolize for the merchant?

4. Santiago is reunited with Fatima at the end of the novel. What does waiting show about her character?

5. What do you suppose might be the source of Santiago's discontent in the seminary that eventually leads him to become a shepherd? What does he hope to learn? What is significant about the boy's choice of occupation?

IV. Vocabulary

____ 1. CONTEMPLATE A. Expressing sorrow or regret

____ 2. PROPRIETOR B. Exert oneself vigorously; try hard

____ 3. ZENITH C. Wearisome uniformity or lack of variety

____ 4. TINGED D. Running at a quick pace

____ 5. LAMENTING E. Hills or ridges of wind-blown sand

____ 6. RUEFULLY F. Seemingly prearranged event that is merely accidental

____ 7. DISEMBARK G. A point on the celestial sphere vertically above a given position

____ 8. CARAVANS H. Close observations of a person or group

____ 9. COINCIDENCE I. Excited; disturbed

____ 10. SURVEILLANCE J. Excessive excitement or enthusiasm; craze

____ 11. MANIA K. To consider thoroughly; think fully or deeply about

____ 12. FAMINE L. Groups that travel together across the desert or through hostile territory for safety

____ 13. SCABBARD M. Sheath for a sword

____ 14. OASIS N. Extreme and general scarcity of food, as within a country

____ 15. MONOTONY O. Torn or ragged clothing

____ 16. AGITATED P. A slight degree of coloration

____ 17. DUNES Q. The owner of a business establishment

____ 18. STRIVE R. To exit a vehicle of transportation

____ 19. SCUTTLING S. In a manner showing or expressing sorrow or pity; mournfully

____ 20. TATTERS T. Small fertile or green area in a desert region

The Alchemist MULTIPLE CHOICE UNIT TEST 1 Answer Key

I. Matching/Identify

N	1.	SANTIAGO	A.	Helps the boy in the market place after he is robbed; ___ seller
R	2.	PRIEST	B.	Tells the boy what his dream means
C	3.	SHEPHERD	C.	Occupation chosen by the boy
S	4.	DREAM	D.	Merchant's unvisited Pilgrimage destination
B	5.	GYPSY	E.	Tells the boy to show him where there is life in the desert
H	6.	SALEM	F.	She waits for the boy's return.
A	7.	CANDY	G.	The boy's help greatly increases his business; ___ Merchant
G	8.	CRYSTAL	H.	The old man who knew all about the boy; King of ___
F	9.	FATIMA	I.	The principle of favorability; beginner's ___
O	10.	ENGLISHMAN	J.	Continent over which the boy travels
M	11.	NARCISSUS	K.	Hooded men of the desert who provide information
I	12.	LUCK	L.	Country where the boy's journey begins
Q	13.	SWORD	M.	For whom the lake weeps
K	14.	BEDOUINS	N.	The boy
T	15.	JOSEPH	O.	Befriends the boy in the caravan
E	16.	ALCHEMIST	P.	Boy's destination based on his dream
P	17.	PYRAMIDS	Q.	Sight of the distracted boy in the marketplace
J	18.	AFRICA	R.	Occupation the boy's parents chose for him
L	19.	SPAIN	S.	This leads the boy to begin his journey
D	20.	MECCA	T.	Boy who saved Egypt through dream interpretation

II. Multiple Choice

C 1. Why does the lake weep for Narcissus?
- A. Narcissus was brutally murdered.
- B. It is grieving the loss of Narcissus.
- C. It had been able to see its own beauty in Narcissus's eyes; it wants him back.
- D. Narcissus left with a woman and it feels neglected.

C 2. Why does the shepherd decide to see the Gypsy woman?
- A. He wants her to tell him about his father.
- B. He wants her to tell his fortune about the merchant's daughter.
- C. He wants her to interpret a recurring dream.
- D. He wants her to make a love potion to give to the merchant's daughter.

B 3. According to the old man, what is the world's greatest lie?
- A. The world's greatest lie is that people have the free will to do as they wish.
- B. The world's greatest lie is that people's lives are controlled by fate.
- C. The world's greatest lie is that people cannot see into the past or the future.
- D. The world's greatest lie is that people were meant to be happy.

B 4. What is the "principle of favorability" that the old man speaks of?
- A. It is also known as "the survival of the fittest."
- B. It is also known as "beginner's luck."
- C. It is also known as "the will of God."
- D. It is also known as "being in the right place at the right time."

C 5. According to the "wisest of wise men," what is the secret of happiness?
- A. The secret of happiness is to "bloom where you are planted."
- B. The secret of happiness is to be happy for others' fortunes without bitterness.
- C. The secret is to see the world's marvels without forgetting the oil in the spoon.
- D. The secret of happiness is to be happy with what you already have.

A 6. In order to attract more business after working there for one month, what does the boy suggest that the crystal merchant allow him to do?
- A. He asks the merchant to let him build a display case for outside the shop.
- B. He asks the merchant to allow him to place an ad in the local papers.
- C. He asks the merchant to allow him to open a stall in the bazaar.
- D. He asks the merchant to let him paint a large billboard on the main road.

155

B 7. Why does the merchant claim to feel worse than he did before the boy arrived to work for him?
   A. The boy has helped improve business, but the merchant doesn't want the extra work.
   B. The boy has shown him how he could accomplish things, but he hates change.
   C. The merchant's daughter has fallen in love with the boy; he disapproves of it.
   D. The boy is a better seller than the crystal merchant.

A 8. How did the camel driver who befriended the boy come to be in this line of work?
   A. He lost his olive orchard to a flood, and he needed to care for his family.
   B. He left his position in the seminary to be able to see the world as a camel driver.
   C. He was taken as a slave as a child by a group of camel drivers; it's all he knows.
   D. He is from a family of camel drivers.

D 9. What is the "Emerald Tablet"?
   A. It is a jewel in the armor of the old King Salem.
   B. It is a magical stone that turns lead into gold.
   C. It is a rare jewel in the crown of the Egyptian pharaoh.
   D. It is a jewel upon which the most important text of alchemy is inscribed.

D 10. What "omens from the desert" does the boy share with the chieftains of the oasis?
   A. He sees two hawks fighting and then envisioned the oasis in flames.
   B. He uses Urim and Thummim and believes that the oasis is in danger.
   C. He hears the winds speak to him about the tribal wars.
   D. He sees a vision of men with swords attacking the oasis.

C 11. What decision does the head chieftain make about the boy's visions?
   A. He laughs that someone so young could possibly have such visions.
   B. He becomes angry and jails the boy as an enemy spy.
   C. He heeds the boy's warning, yet threatens the boy if they do not come true.
   D. He does not take the boy seriously and ignores him.

A 12. When riding out into the desert, what does the alchemist instruct the boy to show him?
   A. He tells the boy to show him where there is life in the desert.
   B. He tells the boy to show him the way to the Pyramids.
   C. He tells the boy to show him where he first saw the omen that led him to warn the chieftain.
   D. He tells the boy to show him how to use Urim and Thummim.

B 13. Why is the boy disappointed when the alchemist writes in the sand what is inscribed on the Emerald Tablet?
- A. The boy thought it would give him the secret to the Language of the World.
- B. It is written in a code the boy does not understand.
- C. The boy expected to learn how to create the Elixir of Life.
- D. The boy expected to learn how to turn any metal into gold.

D 14. What do the armed tribesmen find in the alchemist's bag?
- A. They find a never-ending supply of food.
- B. They find his books on alchemy.
- C. They find the boy's pouch filled with gold.
- D. They find a small flask of liquid and a yellow glass egg.

C 15. What does the desert ask the boy to explain to it?
- A. It wants to know how to turn lead into gold.
- B. It wants to know the Language of the World.
- C. It wants to know what love is.
- D. It wants to know the meaning of life.

B 16. What is the chief's plan for the two men who wanted to end the bet with the boy?
- A. He plans to replace them with the boy and the alchemist.
- B. He plans to remove them from their positions because they were afraid.
- C. He plans to execute them for their fears.
- D. He plans to reward them for not playing into the boy's hand.

C 17. According to the boy, why does alchemy exist?
- A. Alchemy exists to prove that man can create gold from meaningless metals.
- B. Alchemy exists in order to distinguish between those who are searching for the truth and those who are merely greedy.
- C. Alchemy exists so that everyone will search for and find his treasure, and hopefully lead a better life.
- D. Alchemy exists so that everyone can be rich.

A 18. Describe the dream the alchemist tells to the boy.
- A. The alchemist tells the dream of a Roman man about his two sons.
- B. The alchemist says that he had dreamed about a boy who would come to him and then turn himself into the wind.
- C. The alchemist reiterates the boy's dream from the sacristy in Spain.
- D. The alchemist says that he dreamed that he saw the boy at the Great Pyramids.

B 19.　　What warning does the boy's heart whisper as he is about to climb a large dune?
　　　　A. His heart warns him not to climb the dune because danger lurks behind.
　　　　B. His heart warns him to be aware of the place where he is brought to tears.
　　　　C. His heart warns him against greed once he finds his treasure.
　　　　D. His heart warns him not to trust anyone he meets on the other side of the dune.

B 20.　　What piece of advice does the leader of the refugees give the boy before he leaves?
　　　　A. Never be alone in the desert after dark.
　　　　B. Don't bother with dreams; he wasn't stupid enough to go to another country because of a dream.
　　　　C. The boy should hurry back to the oasis before Fatima marries another.
　　　　D. Don't tell anyone what he knows about the Language of the World.

IV. Vocabulary

K	1.	CONTEMPLATE	A.	Expressing sorrow or regret
Q	2.	PROPRIETOR	B.	Exert oneself vigorously; try hard
G	3.	ZENITH	C.	Wearisome uniformity or lack of variety
P	4.	TINGED	D.	Running at a quick pace
A	5.	LAMENTING	E.	Hills or ridges of wind-blown sand
S	6.	RUEFULLY	F.	Seemingly prearranged event that is merely accidental
R	7.	DISEMBARK	G.	A point on the celestial sphere vertically above a given position
L	8.	CARAVANS	H.	Close observations of a person or group
F	9.	COINCIDENCE	I.	Excited; disturbed
H	10.	SURVEILLANCE	J.	Excessive excitement or enthusiasm; craze
J	11.	MANIA	K.	To consider thoroughly; think fully or deeply about
N	12.	FAMINE	L.	Groups that travel together across the desert or through hostile territory for safety
M	13.	SCABBARD	M.	Sheath for a sword
T	14.	OASIS	N.	Extreme and general scarcity of food, as within a country
C	15.	MONOTONY	O.	Torn or ragged clothing
I	16.	AGITATED	P.	A slight degree of coloration
E	17.	DUNES	Q.	The owner of a business establishment
B	18.	STRIVE	R.	To exit a vehicle of transportation
D	19.	SCUTTLING	S.	In a manner showing or expressing sorrow or pity; mournfully
O	20.	TATTERS	T.	Small fertile or green area in a desert region

The Alchemist MULTIPLE CHOICE UNIT TEST 2

I. Matching

____ 1. SANTIAGO   A. Hooded men of the desert who provide information
____ 2. PRIEST   B. Boy's destination based on his dream
____ 3. SHEPHERD   C. Boy who saved Egypt through dream interpretation
____ 4. DREAM   D. The principle of favorability; beginner's ___
____ 5. GYPSY   E. This leads the boy to begin his journey
____ 6. SALEM   F. Occupation chosen by the boy
____ 7. CANDY   G. Sight of the distracted boy in the marketplace
____ 8. CRYSTAL   H. Tells the boy what his dream means
____ 9. FATIMA   I. Tells the boy to show him where there is life in the desert
____ 10. ENGLISHMAN   J. Helps the boy in the market place after he is robbed; ___ seller
____ 11. NARCISSUS   K. For whom the lake weeps
____ 12. LUCK   L. She waits for the boy's return.
____ 13. SWORD   M. Befriends the boy in the caravan
____ 14. BEDOUINS   N. The old man who knew all about the boy; King of ___
____ 15. JOSEPH   O. Country where the boy's journey begins
____ 16. ALCHEMIST   P. The boy
____ 17. PYRAMIDS   Q. Occupation the boy's parents chose for him
____ 18. AFRICA   R. Continent over which the boy travels
____ 19. SPAIN   S. Merchant's unvisited Pilgrimage destination
____ 20. MECCA   T. The boy's help greatly increases his business; ___ Merchant

II. Multiple Choice

1. How does the boy spend his time when the merchant told him that the shepherd could not shear his sheep until the afternoon?
    A. He takes his sheep to another merchant.
    B. He spends the time sleeping.
    C. He reads his new book.
    D. He talks with the merchant's daughter.

2. Describe the shepherd boy's recurring dream.
    A. He dreamed about his own death.
    B. He dreamed of becoming a wealthy merchant, but it all turned to dust.
    C. He dreamed about seven thin cows that ate seven fat cows yet grew no bigger.
    D. He dreamed of being taken to the Pyramids and told of a treasure.

3. According to the old man, what is the one great truth on this planet?
    A. Our deepest desires originated in the soul of the universe.
    B. There is no such thing as free will.
    C. All people can see both the past and the present if they are open to it.
    D. People have absolutely no control over their own destinies.

4. What are Urim and Thummim?
    A. They are the "lead sheep" in the boy's flock.
    B. They are two young boys who will accompany the boy to Egypt.
    C. They are two stones used in divination.
    D. They are two men who bought the boy's sheep.

5. After helping the candy seller erect his stall in the plaza, to what realization does the shepherd boy come?
    A. He realizes that he wants to become a seller in the African bazaar.
    B. They speak different languages, yet they are able to understand one another.
    C. The candy seller stole his money when he was working.
    D. The boy who stole his money is the candy seller's son.

6. Why didn't the crystal merchant ever go on a pilgrimage to Mecca?
    A. He didn't want to leave his shop in the hands of others while he was gone.
    B. He never had enough money.
    C. He wanted to go to Rome instead.
    D. He didn't want to leave his family.

7. When the boy tells the merchant that he is going to be leaving to return to his country to buy sheep, he asks for the merchant's blessing. What does the merchant say about the boy's journey home?
    A. He begs the boy not to go because his business is doing so well now.
    B. He tells the boy that his daughter may accompany him to Spain as his wife.
    C. He tells the boy that just as he will never go to Mecca, the boy will not be buying sheep.
    D. He wishes the boy well in his life.

8. What news does the caravan leader learn that causes the members to become more cautious while traveling, especially at night?
    A. A group of prisoners escaped from an Egyptian prison and are in the desert.
    B. There are rumors that the Englishman is a wanted criminal and bounty hunters are looking for him.
    C. There have been rumors of renegade thieves skulking in the desert.
    D. The desert tribes are at war.

9. Who is Fatima?
    A. She is a woman at the oasis. The boy falls in love with her.
    B. She is the crystal merchant's daughter.
    C. She is the boy's camel that he purchased.
    D. She is the boy's mother that he misses terribly.

10. What decision does the head chieftain make about the boy's visions?
    A. He laughs that someone so young could possibly have such visions.
    B. He does not take the boy seriously and ignores him.
    C. He heeds the boy's warning, yet threatens the boy if they do not come true.
    D. He becomes angry and jails the boy as an enemy spy.

11. What words does the alchemist say that echo those of the old king?
    A. "Wherever your heart is, there you will find your treasure."
    B. "It's not what enters men's mouths that's evil. It's what comes out of their mouths that is."
    C. "Love never keeps a man from pursuing his Personal Legend."
    D. "When a person really desires something, all the universe conspires to help that person to realize his dreams."

12. What does the desert come to mean for Fatima?
    A. It came to mean despair because the desert took her love from her.
    B. It comes to mean the hope for the boy's return.
    C. It comes to mean the loss of love.
    D. It comes to mean joy because the desert has brought her love, even though it is only meant for a short time.

13. According to the alchemist, what is worse than suffering?
    A. He says that denying the heart's desire is worse than suffering.
    B. He says the fear of suffering is worse than the suffering itself.
    C. He says that death is worse than suffering.
    D. He says that not following one's Personal Legend is worse than suffering.

14. Why don't the tribesmen take what is in the alchemist's bag?
    A. They think his books are sorcerer's spells, so they refused to touch them.
    B. The alchemist convinces them that the gold is for their tribal leader who needs it to succeed in the wars of the desert.
    C. They don't believe the alchemist when he tells them the truth about the flask and the egg; they merely laugh and go on their way.
    D. They believe the food to be bewitched, and so they run in fear.

15. When asked who taught the boy the language of the desert and wind, what is the boy's reply?
    A. He says that his heart taught him.
    B. He says that Fatima taught him.
    C. He says that experience taught him.
    D. He says that the alchemist taught him.

16. How does the sun claim to know about love?
    A. The sun claims that the wind taught it about love.
    B. The sun claims that it has learned that love is about working together.
    C. The sun claims that it does not know what love is.
    D. The sun claims that it has learned from accidentally destroying what it once loved.

17. What feat does the alchemist perform at the monastery?
    A. He heals the sick monk with the Elixir of Life.
    B. He creates a flask of the Elixir of Life using a tiny sliver of the Philosopher's Stone.
    C. He turns lead into gold with the Philosopher's Stone.
    D. He brings a dead monk back to life with the Elixir of Life.

18. What did the centurion say that was remembered for all time?
    A. The centurion said that only love can heal a wound.
    B. The centurion said that wherever the heart lies, so will your treasure be.
    C. The centurion said that he was not worthy to have a great healer enter his home, but if only the man would say the word, his servant would be healed.
    D. The centurion said that whenever one has a strong desire, the universe will conspire to make it a reality.

19. As the boy wept at the sight that beheld him, what does he notice in the sand?
    A. He notices a flower growing out of the sand and believed that it marks the place of his treasure.
    B. He notices that his tears turned into diamonds once they hit the sand.
    C. He notices scarab beetles scuttling in the sand.
    D. He notices a snake crawling from a hole and he is reminded of how he had once found life in the desert for the alchemist.

20. How does the boy finance his journey back to Spain?
    A. He retrieves the gold that the Alchemist had left for him at the monastery.
    B. He sells sheep.
    C. He sells crystal near the Pyramids.
    D. He works as a caravan leader.

III. Composition
1. Discuss three positive and three negative character traits for Santiago. What do these traits show you about the kind of person the boy is?

2. Explain the role the king of Salem plays in the boy's adventure. What does he represent to Santiago? What about the crystal merchant's role? Fatima's? The Alchemist's?

3. The old man tells the boy that he is the King of Salem. One possibility is that he is the King of Jerusalem. What might be the significance of this? Suppose that the reference is to Salem, Massachusetts. How might the connotation of this city change the significance to the novel? Explain how this could be a source of irony.

4. Explain the symbolism of the boy's dream.

5. How is the meeting with the refugee at the Pyramids a source of irony? How does the boy's original dream play a role in the irony?

IV. Vocabulary

____ 1. IGNORANT A. A sudden feeling of mental or emotional distress or longing
____ 2. PANG B. Phenomena supposed to portend good or evil; prophetic signs
____ 3. OMENS C. Enthusiastically; in a dedicated manner
____ 4. ABASHED D. Remembered or celebrated through all time
____ 5. PERCEIVED E. Harmonious combination of elements
____ 6. OBLIGATIONS F. Guards
____ 7. REFRAINED G. Gloomy state of mind, esp. when habitual or prolonged
____ 8. NOSTALGIA H. Sentimental longing for the happiness of a former place or time
____ 9. EXULTANT I. Became aware of directly through any of the senses
____ 10. SCIMITARS J. Betrayal of a trust or confidence; breach of faith
____ 11. PROHIBITED K. Highly elated; jubilant; triumphant
____ 12. MELANCHOLY L. Ashamed or embarrassed; disconcerted
____ 13. TREASON M. Curved Asian swords with the sharp edge on the convex side
____ 14. PROVERB N. Daring or bold resistance to authority
____ 15. SENTINELS O. Restrained or held back
____ 16. SYMPHONY P. Duties
____ 17. DEFIANCE Q. Forbidden by authority
____ 18. IMMORTAL R. Lacking in knowledge or training; unlearned
____ 19. AVIDLY S. Worn down by scraping or rubbing
____ 20. ABRADED T. Short, popular, usually wise saying or precept

The Alchemist MULTIPLE CHOICE UNIT TEST 2 Answer Key

I. Matching

P	1.	SANTIAGO	A.	Hooded men of the desert who provide information
Q	2.	PRIEST	B.	Boy's destination based on his dream
F	3.	SHEPHERD	C.	Boy who saved Egypt through dream interpretation
E	4.	DREAM	D.	The principle of favorability; beginner's ___
H	5.	GYPSY	E.	This leads the boy to begin his journey
N	6.	SALEM	F.	Occupation chosen by the boy
J	7.	CANDY	G.	Sight of the distracted boy in the marketplace
T	8.	CRYSTAL	H.	Tells the boy what his dream means
L	9.	FATIMA	I.	Tells the boy to show him where there is life in the desert
M	10.	ENGLISHMAN	J.	Helps the boy in the market place after he is robbed; ___ seller
K	11.	NARCISSUS	K.	For whom the lake weeps
D	12.	LUCK	L.	She waits for the boy's return.
G	13.	SWORD	M.	Befriends the boy in the caravan
A	14.	BEDOUINS	N.	The old man who knew all about the boy; King of ___
C	15.	JOSEPH	O.	Country where the boy's journey begins
I	16.	ALCHEMIST	P.	The boy
B	17.	PYRAMIDS	Q.	Occupation the boy's parents chose for him
R	18.	AFRICA	R.	Continent over which the boy travels
O	19.	SPAIN	S.	Merchant's unvisited Pilgrimage destination
S	20.	MECCA	T.	The boy's help greatly increases his business; ___ Merchant

II. Multiple Choice

D 1. How does the boy spend his time when the merchant told him that the shepherd could not shear his sheep until the afternoon?
   A. He takes his sheep to another merchant.
   B. He spends the time sleeping.
   C. He reads his new book.
   D. He talks with the merchant's daughter.

D 2. Describe the shepherd boy's recurring dream.
   A. He dreamed about his own death.
   B. He dreamed of becoming a wealthy merchant, but it all turned to dust.
   C. He dreamed about seven thin cows that ate seven fat cows yet grew no bigger.
   D. He dreamed of being taken to the Pyramids and told of a treasure.

A 3. According to the old man, what is the one great truth on this planet?
   A. Our deepest desires originated in the soul of the universe.
   B. There is no such thing as free will.
   C. All people can see both the past and the present if they are open to it.
   D. People have absolutely no control over their own destinies.

C 4. What are Urim and Thummim?
   A. They are the "lead sheep" in the boy's flock.
   B. They are two young boys who will accompany the boy to Egypt.
   C. They are two stones used in divination.
   D. They are two men who bought the boy's sheep.

B 5. After helping the candy seller erect his stall in the plaza, to what realization does the shepherd boy come?
   A. He realizes that he wants to become a seller in the African bazaar.
   B. They speak different languages, yet they are able to understand one another.
   C. The candy seller stole his money when he was working.
   D. The boy who stole his money is the candy seller's son.

A 6. Why didn't the crystal merchant ever go on a pilgrimage to Mecca?
   A. He didn't want to leave his shop in the hands of others while he was gone.
   B. He never had enough money.
   C. He wanted to go to Rome instead.
   D. He didn't want to leave his family.

C 7. When the boy tells the merchant that he is going to be leaving to return to his country to buy sheep, he asks for the merchant's blessing. What does the merchant say about the boy's journey home?
- A. He begs the boy not to go because his business is doing so well now.
- B. He tells the boy that his daughter may accompany him to Spain as his wife.
- C. He tells the boy that just as he will never go to Mecca, the boy will not be buying sheep.
- D. He wishes the boy well in his life.

D 8. What news does the caravan leader learn that causes the members to become more cautious while traveling, especially at night?
- A. A group of prisoners escaped from an Egyptian prison and are in the desert.
- B. There are rumors that the Englishman is a wanted criminal and bounty hunters are looking for him.
- C. There have been rumors of renegade thieves skulking in the desert.
- D. The desert tribes are at war.

A 9. Who is Fatima?
- A. She is a woman at the oasis. The boy falls in love with her.
- B. She is the crystal merchant's daughter.
- C. She is the boy's camel that he purchased.
- D. She is the boy's mother that he misses terribly.

C 10. What decision does the head chieftain make about the boy's visions?
- A. He laughs that someone so young could possibly have such visions.
- B. He does not take the boy seriously and ignores him.
- C. He heeds the boy's warning, yet threatens the boy if they do not come true.
- D. He becomes angry and jails the boy as an enemy spy.

D 11. What words does the alchemist say that echo those of the old king?
- A. "Wherever your heart is, there you will find your treasure."
- B. "It's not what enters men's mouths that's evil. It's what comes out of their mouths that is."
- C. "Love never keeps a man from pursuing his Personal Legend."
- D. "When a person really desires something, all the universe conspires to help that person to realize his dreams."

B 12.   What does the desert come to mean for Fatima?
   A. It came to mean despair because the desert took her love from her.
   B. It comes to mean the hope for the boy's return.
   C. It comes to mean the loss of love.
   D. It comes to mean joy because the desert has brought her love, even though it is only meant for a short time.

B 13.   According to the alchemist, what is worse than suffering?
   A. He says that denying the heart's desire is worse than suffering.
   B. He says the fear of suffering is worse than the suffering itself.
   C. He says that death is worse than suffering.
   D. He says that not following one's Personal Legend is worse than suffering.

C 14.   Why don't the tribesmen take what is in the alchemist's bag?
   A. They think his books are sorcerer's spells, so they refused to touch them.
   B. The alchemist convinces them that the gold is for their tribal leader who needs it to succeed in the wars of the desert.
   C. They don't believe the alchemist when he tells them the truth about the flask and the egg; they merely laugh and go on their way.
   D. They believe the food to be bewitched, and so they run in fear.

A 15.   When asked who taught the boy the language of the desert and wind, what is the boy's reply?
   A. He says that his heart taught him.
   B. He says that Fatima taught him.
   C. He says that experience taught him.
   D. He says that the alchemist taught him.

B 16.   How does the sun claim to know about love?
   A. The sun claims that the wind taught it about love.
   B. The sun claims that it has learned that love is about working together.
   C. The sun claims that it does not know what love is.
   D. The sun claims that it has learned from accidentally destroying what it once loved.

C 17.   What feat does the alchemist perform at the monastery?
   A.   He heals the sick monk with the Elixir of Life.
   B.   He creates a flask of the Elixir of Life using a tiny sliver of the Philosopher's Stone.
   C.   He turns lead into gold with the Philosopher's Stone.
   D.   He brings a dead monk back to life with the Elixir of Life.

C 18.   What did the centurion say that was remembered for all time?
   A.   The centurion said that only love can heal a wound.
   B.   The centurion said that wherever the heart lies, so will your treasure be.
   C.   The centurion said that he was not worthy to have a great healer enter his home, but if only the man would say the word, his servant would be healed.
   D.   The centurion said that whenever one has a strong desire, the universe will conspire to make it a reality.

C 19.   As the boy wept at the sight that beheld him, what does he notice in the sand?
   A.   He notices a flower growing out of the sand and believed that it marks the place of his treasure.
   B.   He notices that his tears turned into diamonds once they hit the sand.
   C.   He notices scarab beetles scuttling in the sand.
   D.   He notices a snake crawling from a hole and he is reminded of how he had once found life in the desert for the alchemist.

A 20.   How does the boy finance his journey back to Spain?
   A.   He retrieves the gold that the Alchemist had left for him at the monastery.
   B.   He sells sheep.
   C.   He sells crystal near the Pyramids.
   D.   He works as a caravan leader.

IV. Vocabulary

R	1. IGNORANT	A.	A sudden feeling of mental or emotional distress or longing
A	2. PANG	B.	Phenomena supposed to portend good or evil; prophetic signs
B	3. OMENS	C.	Enthusiastically; in a dedicated manner
L	4. ABASHED	D.	Remembered or celebrated through all time
I	5. PERCEIVED	E.	Harmonious combination of elements
P	6. OBLIGATIONS	F.	Guards
O	7. REFRAINED	G.	Gloomy state of mind, esp. when habitual or prolonged
H	8. NOSTALGIA	H.	Sentimental longing for the happiness of a former place or time
K	9. EXULTANT	I.	Became aware of directly through any of the senses
M	10. SCIMITARS	J.	Betrayal of a trust or confidence; breach of faith
Q	11. PROHIBITED	K.	Highly elated; jubilant; triumphant
G	12. MELANCHOLY	L.	Ashamed or embarrassed; disconcerted
J	13. TREASON	M.	Curved Asian swords with the sharp edge on the convex side
T	14. PROVERB	N.	Daring or bold resistance to authority
F	15. SENTINELS	O.	Restrained or held back
E	16. SYMPHONY	P.	Duties
N	17. DEFIANCE	Q.	Forbidden by authority
D	18. IMMORTAL	R.	Lacking in knowledge or training; unlearned
C	19. AVIDLY	S.	Worn down by scraping or rubbing
S	20. ABRADED	T.	Short, popular, usually wise saying or precept

UNIT RESOURCE MATERIALS

BULLETIN BOARD IDEAS *The Alchemist*

1. Save one corner of the board for the best of students' *The Alchemist* writing assignments.
2. Take one of the word search puzzles from the extra activities packet and with a marker copy it over in a large size on the bulletin board. Write the clue words to find to one side. Invite students prior to and after class to find the words and circle them on the bulletin board.
3. Write several of the most significant quotations from the book onto the board on brightly colored paper.
4. Make a bulletin board listing the vocabulary words for this unit. As you complete sections of the novel and discuss the vocabulary for each section, write the definitions on the bulletin board. (if your board is one students face frequently, it will help them learn the words.)
5. Make a bulletin board dedicated to the five obligations outlined in the Koran and followed in the Muslim religion.
6. Create a bulletin board dedicated to the author, Paulo Coelho and his other works.
7. Create a bulletin board dedicated to the works read by students as companion pieces which related to legends surrounding The Philosopher's Stone and The Elixir of Life.
8. Create a bulletin board dedicated to dreams and include Langston Hughes's "A Dream Deferred."
9. Make characterization posters that highlight the various traits for the characters in the novel.
10. Create a bulletin board using the artwork that inspires in-class response writing, and display student responses to the paintings.
11. Create a bulletin board dedicated to various forms of divination from the students' non-fiction research.
12. Create a bulletin board dedicated to the Narcissus myth with mini-posters explaining its relationship to the novel.
13. Create a bulletin board outlining the plot of Hans Christian Andersen's short story, "The Philosopher's Stone."
14. Display the students' character journals next to the posters of each character.

RELATED TOPICS *The Alchemist*

1. Alchemy
2. Taoism and the Five Elements
3. Carl Jung
4. Inner Alchemy
5. Alchemical Allegories
6. Indian Alchemy
7. Dream Interpretation
8. Coptic Monastery
9. Pyramids
10. Sycamore Fig Tree
11. Sheep and Shepherds
12. Quintessence
13. Paracelsus
14. Magnum Opus
15. Transmutation
16. Gold
17. Four Classical Elements
18. Jabir ibn Hayyan (Gerber)
19. Wei Boyang
20. Nagarjuna
21. Elixirs
22. Thomas Aquinas
23. Jakob Boehme
24. Caravans

MORE ACTIVITIES *The Alchemist*

1. Have students work together to make a time line chronology of the events in the story. Take a large piece of construction paper and on one wall (or however you can physically arrange it in your room) make the events of the story along it. Students may want to add drawings our cut-out pictures to represent the events (as well as a written statement).
2. Have students design a book cover (front and back inside flaps) for *The Alchemist.*
3. Have students design a bulletin board (ready to be put up; not just sketched) for *The Alchemist*.
4. Have students choose one chapter of the novel (with sufficient dialogue) to rewrite as a play. In conjunction with this assignment, have students write a comparison explaining the difficulties they encountered in changing from one written form to another.
5. Imagine that you are casting a new film about *The Alchemist*. Who would you cast as each of the major characters and why? Make a new movie poster to advertise your film.
6. Create a board game that outlines the journey of Santiago, being sure to include all the stops he made on his journey (don't forget his return journey).
7. Imagine that you are creating *The Alchemist: the Musical.* Have students write appropriate song lyrics for characters that exemplify his/her feelings in the scene. Decide on a musical style for each song (such as a love ballad for Fatima and Santiago) and explain your choice.
8. Ask students to use the journal entries they wrote in class and turn them into a narrative poem about their own Personal Legend.
9. Have students compare Santiago's journey to the journey of another character in literature (such as *The Little Prince*, Dorothy in *The Wizard of Oz*, Bastain in *The Neverending Story*, the Pevensie children in T*he Lion, the Witch, and the Wardrobe*). In each of these examples, the main character(s) encounters fantastical characters such as talking animals and talking objects.
10. Create a newspaper that relates events in *The Alchemist*. You can include editorials, opinion pieces, entertainment, editorial cartoons, human interest stories, etc.

UNIT WORD LIST *The Alchemist*

No.	Word	Clue/Definition
1.	AFRICA	Continent over which the boy travels
2.	ALCHEMIST	Tells the boy to show him where there is life in the desert
3.	BEDOUINS	Hooded men of the desert who provide information
4.	BUTTERFLY	It is a good omen.
5.	CAMEL	Desert transportation
6.	CANDY	Helps the boy in the market place after he is robbed; ___ seller
7.	CENTURION	His words of faith were to be remembered for all time.
8.	COURAGE	Quality most essential to understanding the Language of the World
9.	CRYSTAL	The boy's help greatly increases his business; ___ Merchant
10.	DISPLAY	The boy wants to build one outside the store.
11.	DREAM	This leads the boy to begin his journey
12.	EGYPT	Location of the Pyramids
13.	ELIXIR	Liquid part of the Master Work; ___ of Life
14.	EMERALD	Contains all the important texts of alchemy; ___ Tablet
15.	ENGLISHMAN	Befriends the boy in the caravan
16.	FALCON	Sent out by the alchemist to hunt each day
17.	FATE	The greatest lie: Our lives become controlled by ___.
18.	FATIMA	She waits for the boy's return.
19.	GOLD	The alchemist turned lead into this.
20.	GYPSY	Tells the boy what his dream means
21.	HEART	Alchemist tells the boy to listen to this.
22.	JOSEPH	Boy who saved Egypt through dream interpretation
23.	KORAN	Muslim book of faith
24.	LEGEND	Love never keeps a man from pursuing his Personal ___.
25.	LOVE	Desert asks the boy to explain it.
26.	LUCK	The principle of favorability; beginner's ___
27.	MECCA	Merchant's unvisited Pilgrimage destination
28.	MONK	He holds gold for the boy in case he ever needs it.
29.	NARCISSUS	For whom the lake weeps
30.	OASIS	Fatima's home is there.
31.	PRIEST	Occupation the boy's parents chose for him
32.	PYRAMIDS	Boy's destination based on his dream
33.	READING	Pastime of the Englishman
34.	SALEM	The old man who knew all about the boy; King of ___
35.	SANTIAGO	The boy
36.	SHEEP	The boy works for money to buy these.
37.	SHEPHERD	Occupation chosen by the boy
38.	SOUL	Principle that governs all things; ___ of the World

No.	Word	Clue/Definition
39.	SPAIN	Country where the boy's journey begins
40.	STONE	Solid part of the Master Work; Philosopher's ___
41.	SUFFERING	Fear of this is worse than the thing itself.
42.	SUN	It claims to know about love.
43.	SWORD	Sight of the distracted boy in the marketplace
44.	SYCAMORE	The boy found treasure beneath it; ___ tree.
45.	TEARS	Be aware of the place where you are brought to ___.
46.	TRAVEL	The baker had once desired this.
47.	TRUTH	When one wants to do something, it is because that desire originated in the soul of the universe; the world's greatest ___.
48.	URIM	Divination stones given to the boy; ___ and Thummim
49.	WARS	Tribal ___ take place in the desert.
50.	WIND	Alchemist claims the boy can turn himself into this.

WORD SEARCH - The Alchemist

```
F A L C O N G O L D I S P L A Y V D P S
F S V Q R C D T D A S A N T I A G O C H
B K S Y Z M O D L M B M R E A D I N G T
U C S C D W D U S I S A C I R F A M S R
T Y A Y A L I R R T X E M F Q A N I E T
T T L Z R R C N K A J R O Y W T M R R L
E N E M E R A L D F G D N E G E L U O S
R F M A V K M B Q N R E K V H G G V M B
F K W Q R D E Q I E C K C C V Y E C A R
L N E K Q S L R H G R E L H S P X S C C
Y M N J O S E P H P Y A N K X T W W Y C
S C G S P F E B N Y S P X T O Z A O S Y
P B L Y F H M Y A R T H S G U R P R X Y
A E I U S Y Z M R A A S N Y S R A D D B
I D S H T U R T C M L I T C S P I N D R
N O H W R X P C I I B S R O R U A O I M
L U M W A L E Y S D W A A I N C N X N B
U I A N V M E Q S S L O E X M E I R S X
C N N R E F H F U F Q S H P S L N X C M
K S G G L B S X S M T P O M E N S R Z W
```

AFRICA	EMERALD	MECCA	SOUL
ALCHEMIST	ENGLISHMAN	MONK	SPAIN
BEDOUINS	FALCON	NARCISSUS	STONE
BUTTERFLY	FATE	OASIS	SUFFERING
CAMEL	FATIMA	OMENS	SUN
CANDY	GOLD	PRIEST	SWORD
CENTURION	GYPSY	PYRAMIDS	SYCAMORE
COURAGE	HEART	READING	TEARS
CRYSTAL	JOSEPH	SALEM	TRAVEL
DISPLAY	KORAN	SANTIAGO	TRUTH
DREAM	LEGEND	SCARAB	URIM
EGYPT	LOVE	SHEEP	WARS
ELIXIR	LUCK	SHEPHERD	WIND

WORD SEARCH ANSWER KEY - The Alchemist

AFRICA	EMERALD	MECCA	SOUL
ALCHEMIST	ENGLISHMAN	MONK	SPAIN
BEDOUINS	FALCON	NARCISSUS	STONE
BUTTERFLY	FATE	OASIS	SUFFERING
CAMEL	FATIMA	OMENS	SUN
CANDY	GOLD	PRIEST	SWORD
CENTURION	GYPSY	PYRAMIDS	SYCAMORE
COURAGE	HEART	READING	TEARS
CRYSTAL	JOSEPH	SALEM	TRAVEL
DISPLAY	KORAN	SANTIAGO	TRUTH
DREAM	LEGEND	SCARAB	URIM
EGYPT	LOVE	SHEEP	WARS
ELIXIR	LUCK	SHEPHERD	WIND

CROSSWORD - The Alchemist

Across

1. The boy found treasure beneath it: ___ tree
4. Muslim book of faith
6. Divination stones given to the boy: ___ and Thummim
7. The greatest lie: Our lives become controlled by ___.
8. Tribal ___ are taking place in the desert.
9. Tells the boy to show him where there is life in the desert
14. Liquid part of the Master Work: ___ of Life
17. The boy's help greatly increases the ___ Merchant's business.
18. Desert transportation
22. Merchant's unvisited Pilgrimage destination
23. Country where they boy's journey begins
24. It claims to know about love.
25. Alchemist tells the boy to listen to this.
26. The alchemist turned lead into this.

Down

1. Sacred beetle; good omen
2. Quality most essential to understanding the Language of the World
3. Continent over which the boy travels
5. Pastime of the Englishman
10. His words of faith were to be remembered for all time.
11. Befriends the boy in the caravan
12. Be aware of the place where you are brought to ___.
13. The boy wants to build one outside the store.
15. Sent out by the alchemist to hunt each day
16. Tells the boy what his dream means
19. Contains all the important texts of alchemy: ___ Tablet
20. Fatima's home is there.
21. The old man who knew all about the boy; King of ___

CROSSWORD ANSWER KEY - The Alchemist

Across
1. The boy found treasure beneath it: ___ tree
4. Muslim book of faith
6. Divination stones given to the boy: ___ and Thummim
7. The greatest lie: Our lives become controlled by ___.
8. Tribal ___ are taking place in the desert.
9. Tells the boy to show him where there is life in the desert
14. Liquid part of the Master Work: ___ of Life
17. The boy's help greatly increases the ___ Merchant's business.
18. Desert transportation
22. Merchant's unvisited Pilgrimage destination
23. Country where they boy's journey begins
24. It claims to know about love.
25. Alchemist tells the boy to listen to this.
26. The alchemist turned lead into this.

Down
1. Sacred beetle; good omen
2. Quality most essential to understanding the Language of the World
3. Continent over which the boy travels
5. Pastime of the Englishman
10. His words of faith were to be remembered for all time.
11. Befriends the boy in the caravan
12. Be aware of the place where you are brought to ___.
13. The boy wants to build one outside the store.
15. Sent out by the alchemist to hunt each day
16. Tells the boy what his dream means
19. Contains all the important texts of alchemy: ___ Tablet
20. Fatima's home is there.
21. The old man who knew all about the boy; King of ___

MATCHING 1 *The Alchemist*

____ 1. SANTIAGO   A. He holds gold for the boy in case he ever needs it.

____ 2. PYRAMIDS   B. Alchemist tells the boy to listen to this.

____ 3. HEART   C. Contains all the important texts of alchemy; ___ Tablet

____ 4. CENTURION   D. Boy's destination based on his dream

____ 5. MONK   E. The greatest lie: Our lives become controlled by ___.

____ 6. FATE   F. Merchant's unvisited Pilgrimage destination

____ 7. MECCA   G. For whom the lake weeps

____ 8. OASIS   H. Tells the boy what his dream means

____ 9. FALCON   I. Helps the boy in the market place after he is robbed; ___ seller

____ 10. JOSEPH   J. Occupation chosen by the boy

____ 11. STONE   K. Sent out by the alchemist to hunt each day

____ 12. SHEPHERD   L. His words of faith were to be remembered for all time.

____ 13. GYPSY   M. She waits for the boy's return.

____ 14. CANDY   N. The boy found treasure beneath it; ___ tree.

____ 15. FATIMA   O. Boy who saved Egypt through dream interpretation

____ 16. NARCISSUS   P. Solid part of the Master Work; Philosopher's ___

____ 17. URIM   Q. The boy

____ 18. SYCAMORE   R. Divination stones given to the boy; ___ and Thummim

____ 19. EMERALD   S. It claims to know about love.

____ 20. SUN   T. Fatima's home is there.

MATCHING 1 ANSWER KEY *The Alchemist*

Q	1.	SANTIAGO	A.	He holds gold for the boy in case he ever needs it.
D	2.	PYRAMIDS	B.	Alchemist tells the boy to listen to this.
B	3.	HEART	C.	Contains all the important texts of alchemy; ___ Tablet
L	4.	CENTURION	D.	Boy's destination based on his dream
A	5.	MONK	E.	The greatest lie: Our lives become controlled by ___.
E	6.	FATE	F.	Merchant's unvisited Pilgrimage destination
F	7.	MECCA	G.	For whom the lake weeps
T	8.	OASIS	H.	Tells the boy what his dream means
K	9.	FALCON	I.	Helps the boy in the market place after he is robbed; ___ seller
O	10.	JOSEPH	J.	Occupation chosen by the boy
P	11.	STONE	K.	Sent out by the alchemist to hunt each day
J	12.	SHEPHERD	L.	His words of faith were to be remembered for all time.
H	13.	GYPSY	M.	She waits for the boy's return.
I	14.	CANDY	N.	The boy found treasure beneath it; ___ tree.
M	15.	FATIMA	O.	Boy who saved Egypt through dream interpretation
G	16.	NARCISSUS	P.	Solid part of the Master Work; Philosopher's ___
R	17.	URIM	Q.	The boy
N	18.	SYCAMORE	R.	Divination stones given to the boy; ___ and Thummim
C	19.	EMERALD	S.	It claims to know about love.
S	20.	SUN	T.	Fatima's home is there.

MATCHING 2 *The Alchemist*

____ 1. PRIEST   A. Continent over which the boy travels

____ 2. AFRICA   B. It is a good omen.

____ 3. WIND   C. The old man who knew all about the boy; King of ___

____ 4. SPAIN   D. The principle of favorability; beginner's ___

____ 5. SHEEP   E. Quality most essential to understanding the Language of the World

____ 6. BUTTERFLY   F. Hooded men of the desert who provide information

____ 7. SOUL   G. Befriends the boy in the caravan

____ 8. LEGEND   H. Occupation the boy's parents chose for him

____ 9. LOVE   I. The boy works for money to buy these.

____ 10. ALCHEMIST   J. Liquid part of the Master Work; ___ of Life

____ 11. COURAGE   K. The boy's help greatly increases his business; ___ Merchant

____ 12. DREAM   L. Country where the boy's journey begins

____ 13. SALEM   M. This leads the boy to begin his journey

____ 14. CRYSTAL   N. Love never keeps a man from pursuing his Personal ___.

____ 15. ENGLISHMAN   O. Desert asks the boy to explain it.

____ 16. LUCK   P. Principle that governs all things; ___ of the World

____ 17. SWORD   Q. Be aware of the place where you are brought to ___.

____ 18. BEDOUINS   R. Tells the boy to show him where there is life in the desert

____ 19. ELIXIR   S. Sight of the distracted boy in the marketplace

____ 20. TEARS   T. Alchemist claims the boy can turn himself into this.

MATCHING 2 ANSWER KEY *The Alchemist*

H	1.	PRIEST	A.	Continent over which the boy travels
A	2.	AFRICA	B.	It is a good omen.
T	3.	WIND	C.	The old man who knew all about the boy; King of ___
L	4.	SPAIN	D.	The principle of favorability; beginner's ___
I	5.	SHEEP	E.	Quality most essential to understanding the Language of the World
B	6.	BUTTERFLY	F.	Hooded men of the desert who provide information
P	7.	SOUL	G.	Befriends the boy in the caravan
N	8.	LEGEND	H.	Occupation the boy's parents chose for him
O	9.	LOVE	I.	The boy works for money to buy these.
R	10.	ALCHEMIST	J.	Liquid part of the Master Work; ___ of Life
E	11.	COURAGE	K.	The boy's help greatly increases his business; ___ Merchant
M	12.	DREAM	L.	Country where the boy's journey begins
C	13.	SALEM	M.	This leads the boy to begin his journey
K	14.	CRYSTAL	N.	Love never keeps a man from pursuing his Personal ___.
G	15.	ENGLISHMAN	O.	Desert asks the boy to explain it.
D	16.	LUCK	P.	Principle that governs all things; ___ of the World
S	17.	SWORD	Q.	Be aware of the place where you are brought to ___.
F	18.	BEDOUINS	R.	Tells the boy to show him where there is life in the desert
J	19.	ELIXIR	S.	Sight of the distracted boy in the marketplace
Q	20.	TEARS	T.	Alchemist claims the boy can turn himself into this.

JUGGLE LETTERS 1 *The Alchemist*

_____ = 1. TGSIAANO
The boy

_____ = 2. OLFNAC
Sent out by the alchemist to hunt each day

_____ = 3. EELGND
Love never keeps a man from pursuing his Personal ___.

_____ = 4. ISOSA
Fatima's home is there.

_____ = 5. CCMAE
Merchant's unvisited Pilgrimage destination

_____ = 6. IBUDENOS
Hooded men of the desert who provide information

_____ = 7. SMORYCAE
The boy found treasure beneath it; ___ tree.

_____ = 8. MRIU
Divination stones given to the boy; ___ and Thummim

_____ = 9. SACSINUSR
For whom the lake weeps

_____ = 10. FATIMA
She waits for the boy's return.

_____ = 11. CAYSLTR
The boy's help greatly increases his business; ___ Merchant

_____ = 12. EMLSA
The old man who knew all about the boy; King of ___

_____ = 13. YSYGP
Tells the boy what his dream means

_____ = 14. PHEEHDRS
Occupation chosen by the boy

_____ = 15. NKARO
Muslim book of faith

JUGGLE LETTERS 1 ANSWER KEY *The Alchemist*

SANTIAGO	= 1.	TGSIAANO
		The boy
FALCON	= 2.	OLFNAC
		Sent out by the alchemist to hunt each day
LEGEND	= 3.	EELGND
		Love never keeps a man from pursuing his Personal ___.
OASIS	= 4.	ISOSA
		Fatima's home is there.
MECCA	= 5.	CCMAE
		Merchant's unvisited Pilgrimage destination
BEDOUINS	= 6.	IBUDENOS
		Hooded men of the desert who provide information
SYCAMORE	= 7.	SMORYCAE
		The boy found treasure beneath it; ___ tree.
URIM	= 8.	MRIU
		Divination stones given to the boy; ___ and Thummim
NARCISSUS	= 9.	SACSINUSR
		For whom the lake weeps
FATIMA	= 10.	FATIMA
		She waits for the boy's return.
CRYSTAL	= 11.	CAYSLTR
		The boy's help greatly increases his business; ___ Merchant
SALEM	= 12.	EMLSA
		The old man who knew all about the boy; King of ___
GYPSY	= 13.	YSYGP
		Tells the boy what his dream means
SHEPHERD	= 14.	PHEEHDRS
		Occupation chosen by the boy
KORAN	= 15.	NKARO
		Muslim book of faith

JUGGLE LETTERS 2 *The Alchemist*

_____ = 1. ANITGOSA
                      The boy

_____ = 2. LFTURTBYE
                      It is a good omen.

_____ = 3. ESPEH
                      The boy works for money to buy these.

_____ = 4. ORECNNIUT
                      His words of faith were to be remembered for all time.

_____ = 5. FIACAR
                      Continent over which the boy travels

_____ = 6. MAIYDSPR
                      Boy's destination based on his dream

_____ = 7. ACHEMLTIS
                      Tells the boy to show him where there is life in the desert

_____ = 8. JPESHO
                      Boy who saved Egypt through dream interpretation

_____ = 9. CUERGOA
                      Quality most essential to understanding the Language of the World

_____ = 10. TENOS
                      Solid part of the Master Work; Philosopher's ___

_____ = 11. IXLIRE
                      Liquid part of the Master Work; ___ of Life

_____ = 12. NDISEUBO
                      Hooded men of the desert who provide information

_____ = 13. RNCSSISUA
                      For whom the lake weeps

_____ = 14. PYSGY
                      Tells the boy what his dream means

_____ = 15. SOAIS
                      Fatima's home is there.

JUGGLE LETTERS 2 ANSWER KEY *The Alchemist*

SANTIAGO	= 1.	ANITGOSA The boy
BUTTERFLY	= 2.	LFTURTBYE It is a good omen.
SHEEP	= 3.	ESPEH The boy works for money to buy these.
CENTURION	= 4.	ORECNNIUT His words of faith were to be remembered for all time.
AFRICA	= 5.	FIACAR Continent over which the boy travels
PYRAMIDS	= 6.	MAIYDSPR Boy's destination based on his dream
ALCHEMIST	= 7.	ACHEMLTIS Tells the boy to show him where there is life in the desert
JOSEPH	= 8.	JPESHO Boy who saved Egypt through dream interpretation
COURAGE	= 9.	CUERGOA Quality most essential to understanding the Language of the World
STONE	= 10.	TENOS Solid part of the Master Work; Philosopher's ___
ELIXIR	= 11.	IXLIRE Liquid part of the Master Work; ___ of Life
BEDOUINS	= 12.	NDISEUBO Hooded men of the desert who provide information
NARCISSUS	= 13.	RNCSSISUA For whom the lake weeps
GYPSY	= 14.	PYSGY Tells the boy what his dream means
OASIS	= 15.	SOAIS Fatima's home is there.

VOCABULARY RESOURCE MATERIALS

The Alchemist Vocabulary

No.	Word	Clue/Definition
1.	ABASHED	Ashamed or embarrassed; disconcerted
2.	ABRADED	Worn down by scraping or rubbing
3.	AGITATED	Excited; disturbed
4.	ALCHEMY	Medieval philosophy concerned with transmuting common substances into something of value
5.	AVIDLY	Enthusiastically; in a dedicated manner
6.	CAPRICIOUS	Subject to whim; impulsive and unpredictable
7.	CARAVANS	Groups that travel together across the desert or through hostile territory for safety
8.	CENTURION	Commander of a century in the Roman army
9.	COINCIDENCE	Seemingly prearranged event that is merely accidental
10.	COMMENCED	Began
11.	COMMISSION	Percentage of a sales price allowed to sales representatives for their services
12.	CONTEMPLATE	To consider thoroughly; think fully or deeply about
13.	DEFIANCE	Daring or bold resistance to authority
14.	DISEMBARK	To exit a vehicle of transportation
15.	DROUGHT	A period of dry weather, esp. a long one that is injurious to crops
16.	DUNES	Hills or ridges of wind-blown sand
17.	ELIXIR	Sweetened mixture of alcohol and water containing medicines
18.	EVOLVED	Developed gradually
19.	EXPEDITION	Excursion, journey, or voyage made for some specific purpose
20.	EXULTANT	Highly elated; jubilant; triumphant
21.	FAMINE	Extreme and general scarcity of food, as within a country
22.	HANDWROUGHT	Made by hand
23.	IGNORANT	Lacking in knowledge or training; unlearned
24.	IMMERSE	To involve deeply; soak; sink totally into
25.	IMMORTAL	Remembered or celebrated through all time
26.	INCESSANTLY	Continually; without a break
27.	INFIDELS	Unbelievers with respect to a particular religion
28.	INSISTENTLY	In a manner compelling attention or notice
29.	INTUITIVELY	Through natural insight; without learning
30.	INVOKED	Caused, called forth, or brought about
31.	IRRITATING	Exciting to impatience or anger; annoying
32.	LAMENTING	Expressing sorrow or regret
33.	LEVANTER	Strong easterly wind in the Mediterranean
34.	LIMITATIONS	Shortcomings or defects
35.	LUMINOUS	Brilliant intellectually; enlightening

No.	Word	Clue/Definition
36.	MANIA	Excessive excitement or enthusiasm; craze
37.	MELANCHOLY	Gloomy state of mind, esp. when habitual or prolonged
38.	MIRAGES	Optical illusions in sandy deserts caused by hot air
39.	MONOTONY	Wearisome uniformity or lack of variety
40.	NOCTURNAL	Of or pertaining to the night
41.	NOSTALGIA	Sentimental longing for the happiness of a former place or time
42.	OASIS	Small fertile or green area in a desert region
43.	OBJECTIVE	Not influenced by personal feelings; based on facts; unbiased
44.	OBLIGATIONS	Duties
45.	OMENS	Phenomena supposed to portend good or evil; prophetic signs
46.	ORIGINATED	Brought into being; created
47.	PANG	A sudden feeling of mental or emotional distress or longing
48.	PERCEIVED	Became aware of directly through any of the senses
49.	PHARAOH	Title of an ancient Egyptian King
50.	PRECONCEIVED	Forming an opinion before possessing full knowledge
51.	PROGNOSTICATIONS	Forecasts or predictions
52.	PROHIBITED	Forbidden by authority
53.	PROJECTED	Thrown forward
54.	PROPRIETOR	The owner of a business establishment
55.	PROVERB	Short, popular, usually wise saying or precept
56.	PYRAMIDS	Pyramid-shaped stone structures in Egypt housing the tombs of great Egyptian leaders
57.	REACCUSTOMED	Re-familiarized after having stopped a practice or habit
58.	REFRAINED	Restrained or held back
59.	REFUGE	Shelter or protection from danger or trouble
60.	RUEFULLY	In a manner showing or expressing sorrow or pity; mournfully
61.	SACRISTY	A room in a church housing the sacred vessels and vestments
62.	SCABBARD	Sheath for a sword
63.	SCARAB	Type of beetle held sacred by the Ancient Egyptians
64.	SCIMITARS	Curved Asian swords with the sharp edge on the convex side
65.	SCUTTLING	Running at a quick pace
66.	SENTINELS	Guards
67.	STRIVE	Exert oneself vigorously; try hard
68.	SURVEILLANCE	Close observations of a person or group
69.	SYMPHONY	Harmonious combination of elements
70.	TATTERS	Torn or ragged clothing

No.	Word	Clue/Definition
71.	TETHERS	Ropes, chains, or similar restraints for holding an animal in place
72.	TINGED	A slight degree of coloration
73.	TRACTS	Pamphlets containing a religious or political declaration or appeal
74.	TRAJECTORY	Path of a projectile or other moving body through space
75.	TRANSMITTED	Passed; transferred
76.	TREASON	Betrayal of a trust or confidence; breach of faith
77.	ZENITH	A point on the celestial sphere vertically above a given position

VOCABULARY WORD SEARCH - The Alchemist

```
I M M E R S E Q L M T P W K V H C S S M
E W K C U N B A P L H S R E H T E T C T
V J G Y E L N A C B A S O O X I V R U W
O H W R F R N S N S D M M H V N S I T G
L D R O U G H T C O M M E N C E D V T K
V E B T L T I I O A S C N N C Z R E L C
E K C C L M M E I S R T S N T M I B I S
D O H E Y I M L N I M A A Z K I G Y N W
N V L J T R O I C S E L B L S R N Y G N
F N T A A A R X I L L C S E G R O G P L
A I R R V G T I D I A A C V T I R M E P
M S A T I E A R E M N R A A A T A O R D
I D N M D S L V N I C A B N T A N C S
N I S A L M R D C T H V B T T T T O E Y
E M M N Y U T E E A O A A E E I R T I Q
L A I I S P R H Z T L N R R R N E O V V
C R T A M T A S G I Y S D F S G A N E W
H Y T S I R C A S O D U N E S Y S Y D L
M P E Y R Z T B I N F I D E L S O R C L
Y Q D G L Q S A S S D H L U M I N O U S
```

ABASHED	LAMENTING	RUEFULLY
AVIDLY	LEVANTER	SACRISTY
CARAVANS	LIMITATIONS	SCABBARD
COINCIDENCE	LUMINOUS	SCARAB
COMMENCED	MANIA	SCIMITARS
DROUGHT	MELANCHOLY	SCUTTLING
DUNES	MIRAGES	STRIVE
ELIXIR	MONOTONY	SURVEILLANCE
EVOLVED	NOCTURNAL	TATTERS
FAMINE	NOSTALGIA	TETHERS
IGNORANT	OASIS	TINGED
IMMERSE	OMENS	TRACTS
IMMORTAL	PANG	TRAJECTORY
INFIDELS	PERCEIVED	TRANSMITTED
INVOKED	PROVERB	TREASON
IRRITATING	PYRAMIDS	ZENITH

VOCABULARY WORD SEARCH ANSWER KEY - The Alchemist

```
I  M  M  E  R  S  E     L        P                       H        S     S
E              U           A  P        S  R  E  H  T  E  T        C
V              Y     A  N        A           O  O        I     R     U
O              R  F  N  S  N  S        M        V  N        R        T
L  D  R  O  U  G  H  T  C  O  M  M  E  N  C  E  D        I  V     T
V  E        T     T  I  O  A  S        N  N  C  Z     R     E     L
E  K  C     L  M  E  I  S  S     R  T  S  N  T        I  B     L
D  O     E  Y  I  M  L  N  I  M  A     L        I  G        I  N
N  V  J  T  R  O  I  C  S  E  L  B     R  N           G     P
F  N  T  A  A  R  X  I  L  L  C  S  E  G  R  O  G     E
A  I  R  R  V  G  T  I  D  I  A  A  C  V  T  I  R  M
M  S  A  T  I  E  A  R  E  M  N  R  A  A  T  A  O  R  D
I  D  N  M  D  S  L  V  N  I  C  A  B  N  T  A  N  O  C
N  I  S  A  L     R  D  C  T  H  V  B  T  T  T  O  E
E  M  M  N  Y  U  T  E  E  A  O  A  A  E  I  N  T  I
   A  I  I  S     R  H  T  L  N  R  R  R  E  R  O  V
   R  T  A        A  S  I  Y  S  D     S  G  A  N  E
   Y  T  S  I  R  C  A  S  O  D  U  N  E  S  S  Y  D
   P  E                 T  B  I  N  F  I  D  E  L  S  O
      D              S  A     S           L  U  M  I  N  O  U  S
```

ABASHED	LAMENTING	RUEFULLY
AVIDLY	LEVANTER	SACRISTY
CARAVANS	LIMITATIONS	SCABBARD
COINCIDENCE	LUMINOUS	SCARAB
COMMENCED	MANIA	SCIMITARS
DROUGHT	MELANCHOLY	SCUTTLING
DUNES	MIRAGES	STRIVE
ELIXIR	MONOTONY	SURVEILLANCE
EVOLVED	NOCTURNAL	TATTERS
FAMINE	NOSTALGIA	TETHERS
IGNORANT	OASIS	TINGED
IMMERSE	OMENS	TRACTS
IMMORTAL	PANG	TRAJECTORY
INFIDELS	PERCEIVED	TRANSMITTED
INVOKED	PROVERB	TREASON
IRRITATING	PYRAMIDS	ZENITH

VOCABULARY CROSSWORD - The Alchemist

Across
1. Small fertile or green area in a desert region
3. Path of a projectile or other moving body through space
5. Short, popular, usually wise saying or precept
7. In a manner showing or expressing sorrow or pity; mournfully
11. Sudden feeling of mental or emotional distress or longing
13. Gloomy state of mind, esp. when prolonged
15. Type of beetle held sacred by the Ancient Egyptians
19. Point on the celestial sphere vertically above a given position
20. Of or pertaining to the night
21. Caused, called forth, or brought about
22. Slight degree of coloration

Down
1. Prophetic signs
2. Close observations of a person or group
3. Betrayal of a trust or confidence; breach of faith
4. Duties
6. Shelter or protection from danger or trouble
8. Strong easterly wind in the Mediterranean
9. Lacking in knowledge or training; unlearned
10. Passed; transferred
12. Curved Asian swords
13. Wearisome uniformity or lack of variety
14. Became aware of directly through the senses
16. Try hard; exert oneself vigorously
17. Hills or ridges of wind-blown sand
18. Excessive excitement or enthusiasm; craze

VOCABULARY CROSSWORD ANSWER KEY - The Alchemist

Across
1. Small fertile or green area in a desert region
3. Path of a projectile or other moving body through space
5. Short, popular, usually wise saying or precept
7. In a manner showing or expressing sorrow or pity; mournfully
11. Sudden feeling of mental or emotional distress or longing
13. Gloomy state of mind, esp. when prolonged
15. Type of beetle held sacred by the Ancient Egyptians
19. Point on the celestial sphere vertically above a given position
20. Of or pertaining to the night
21. Caused, called forth, or brought about
22. Slight degree of coloration

Down
1. Prophetic signs
2. Close observations of a person or group
3. Betrayal of a trust or confidence; breach of faith
4. Duties
6. Shelter or protection from danger or trouble
8. Strong easterly wind in the Mediterranean
9. Lacking in knowledge or training; unlearned
10. Passed; transferred
12. Curved Asian swords
13. Wearisome uniformity or lack of variety
14. Became aware of directly through the senses
16. Try hard; exert oneself vigorously
17. Hills or ridges of wind-blown sand
18. Excessive excitement or enthusiasm; craze

VOCABULARY MATCHING 1 *The Alchemist*

____ 1. TRANSMITTED   A. Seemingly prearranged event that is merely accidental

____ 2. IRRITATING   B. Forming an opinion before possessing full knowledge

____ 3. INFIDELS   C. Passed; transferred

____ 4. IGNORANT   D. Wearisome uniformity or lack of variety

____ 5. EXULTANT   E. Ashamed or embarrassed; disconcerted

____ 6. DUNES   F. Not influenced by personal feelings; based on facts; unbiased

____ 7. CONTEMPLATE   G. Shelter or protection from danger or trouble

____ 8. COINCIDENCE   H. Enthusiastically; in a dedicated manner

____ 9. AVIDLY   I. Ropes, chains, or similar restraints for holding an animal in place

____ 10. LUMINOUS   J. Exciting to impatience or anger; annoying

____ 11. MONOTONY   K. A sudden feeling of mental or emotional distress or longing

____ 12. TETHERS   L. Brilliant intellectually; enlightening

____ 13. STRIVE   M. To consider thoroughly; think fully or deeply about

____ 14. SCARAB   N. Unbelievers with respect to a particular religion

____ 15. REFUGE   O. Short, popular, usually wise saying or precept

____ 16. PROVERB   P. Hills or ridges of wind-blown sand

____ 17. PRECONCEIVED   Q. Exert oneself vigorously; try hard

____ 18. PANG   R. Lacking in knowledge or training; unlearned

____ 19. OBJECTIVE   S. Highly elated; jubilant; triumphant

____ 20. ABASHED   T. Type of beetle held sacred by the Ancient Egyptians

VOCABULARY MATCHING 1 ANSWER KEY *The Alchemist*

C	1.	TRANSMITTED	A.	Seemingly prearranged event that is merely accidental
J	2.	IRRITATING	B.	Forming an opinion before possessing full knowledge
N	3.	INFIDELS	C.	Passed; transferred
R	4.	IGNORANT	D.	Wearisome uniformity or lack of variety
S	5.	EXULTANT	E.	Ashamed or embarrassed; disconcerted
P	6.	DUNES	F.	Not influenced by personal feelings; based on facts; unbiased
M	7.	CONTEMPLATE	G.	Shelter or protection from danger or trouble
A	8.	COINCIDENCE	H.	Enthusiastically; in a dedicated manner
H	9.	AVIDLY	I.	Ropes, chains, or similar restraints for holding an animal in place
L	10.	LUMINOUS	J.	Exciting to impatience or anger; annoying
D	11.	MONOTONY	K.	A sudden feeling of mental or emotional distress or longing
I	12.	TETHERS	L.	Brilliant intellectually; enlightening
Q	13.	STRIVE	M.	To consider thoroughly; think fully or deeply about
T	14.	SCARAB	N.	Unbelievers with respect to a particular religion
G	15.	REFUGE	O.	Short, popular, usually wise saying or precept
O	16.	PROVERB	P.	Hills or ridges of wind-blown sand
B	17.	PRECONCEIVED	Q.	Exert oneself vigorously; try hard
K	18.	PANG	R.	Lacking in knowledge or training; unlearned
F	19.	OBJECTIVE	S.	Highly elated; jubilant; triumphant
E	20.	ABASHED	T.	Type of beetle held sacred by the Ancient Egyptians

VOCABULARY MATCHING 2 *The Alchemist*

____ 1. TREASON   A. Pyramid-shaped stone structures in Egypt housing the tombs of great Egyptian leaders

____ 2. LAMENTING   B. Close observations of a person or group

____ 3. INSISTENTLY   C. To involve deeply; soak; sink totally into

____ 4. IMMERSE   D. Sweetened mixture of alcohol and water containing medicines

____ 5. FAMINE   E. Of or pertaining to the night

____ 6. ELIXIR   F. Forbidden by authority

____ 7. DEFIANCE   G. Subject to whim; impulsive and unpredictable

____ 8. COMMENCED   H. Betrayal of a trust or confidence; breach of faith

____ 9. CAPRICIOUS   I. Expressing sorrow or regret

____ 10. MANIA   J. Duties

____ 11. NOCTURNAL   K. Extreme and general scarcity of food, as within a country

____ 12. TINGED   L. A slight degree of coloration

____ 13. SURVEILLANCE   M. Began

____ 14. SCIMITARS   N. Daring or bold resistance to authority

____ 15. RUEFULLY   O. Became aware of directly through any of the senses

____ 16. PYRAMIDS   P. Curved Asian swords with the sharp edge on the convex side

____ 17. PROHIBITED   Q. Worn down by scraping or rubbing

____ 18. PERCEIVED   R. In a manner showing or expressing sorrow or pity; mournfully

____ 19. OBLIGATIONS   S. Excessive excitement or enthusiasm; craze

____ 20. ABRADED   T. In a manner compelling attention or notice

VOCABULARY MATCHING 2 ANSWER KEY *The Alchemist*

H	1.	TREASON	A.	Pyramid-shaped stone structures in Egypt housing the tombs of great Egyptian leaders
I	2.	LAMENTING	B.	Close observations of a person or group
T	3.	INSISTENTLY	C.	To involve deeply; soak; sink totally into
C	4.	IMMERSE	D.	Sweetened mixture of alcohol and water containing medicines
K	5.	FAMINE	E.	Of or pertaining to the night
D	6.	ELIXIR	F.	Forbidden by authority
N	7.	DEFIANCE	G.	Subject to whim; impulsive and unpredictable
M	8.	COMMENCED	H.	Betrayal of a trust or confidence; breach of faith
G	9.	CAPRICIOUS	I.	Expressing sorrow or regret
S	10.	MANIA	J.	Duties
E	11.	NOCTURNAL	K.	Extreme and general scarcity of food, as within a country
L	12.	TINGED	L.	A slight degree of coloration
B	13.	SURVEILLANCE	M.	Began
P	14.	SCIMITARS	N.	Daring or bold resistance to authority
R	15.	RUEFULLY	O.	Became aware of directly through any of the senses
A	16.	PYRAMIDS	P.	Curved Asian swords with the sharp edge on the convex side
F	17.	PROHIBITED	Q.	Worn down by scraping or rubbing
O	18.	PERCEIVED	R.	In a manner showing or expressing sorrow or pity; mournfully
J	19.	OBLIGATIONS	S.	Excessive excitement or enthusiasm; craze
Q	20.	ABRADED	T.	In a manner compelling attention or notice

VOCABULARY JUGGLE LETTERS 1 *The Alchemist*

_____ = 1. SENDILFI
Unbelievers with respect to a particular religion

_____ = 2. HEADSAB
Ashamed or embarrassed; disconcerted

_____ = 3. BEDRAAD
Worn down by scraping or rubbing

_____ = 4. ISCPOCIARU
Subject to whim; impulsive and unpredictable

_____ = 5. AANSRVCA
Groups that travel together across the desert or through hostile territory for safety

_____ = 6. NNOECIURT
Commander of a century in the Roman army

_____ = 7. EEOMDMCCN
Began

_____ = 8. EMNETTPCALO
To consider thoroughly; think fully or deeply about

_____ = 9. MIKABDESR
To exit a vehicle of transportation

_____ = 10. EVLOEDV
Developed gradually

_____ = 11. LTXUEANT
Highly elated; jubilant; triumphant

_____ = 12. INMAFE
Extreme and general scarcity of food, as within a country

_____ = 13. RMEEMSI
To involve deeply; soak; sink totally into

_____ = 14. INAESLNTYSC
Continually; without a break

_____ = 15. SRSITCIMA
Curved Asian swords with the sharp edge on the convex side

VOCABULARY JUGGLE LETTERS 1 ANSWER KEY *The Alchemist*

INFIDELS	= 1.	SENDILFI
		Unbelievers with respect to a particular religion
ABASHED	= 2.	HEADSAB
		Ashamed or embarrassed; disconcerted
ABRADED	= 3.	BEDRAAD
		Worn down by scraping or rubbing
CAPRICIOUS	= 4.	ISCPOCIARU
		Subject to whim; impulsive and unpredictable
CARAVANS	= 5.	AANSRVCA
		Groups that travel together across the desert or through hostile territory for safety
CENTURION	= 6.	NNOECIURT
		Commander of a century in the Roman army
COMMENCED	= 7.	EEOMDMCCN
		Began
CONTEMPLATE	= 8.	EMNETTPCALO
		To consider thoroughly; think fully or deeply about
DISEMBARK	= 9.	MIKABDESR
		To exit a vehicle of transportation
EVOLVED	= 10.	EVLOEDV
		Developed gradually
EXULTANT	= 11.	LTXUEANT
		Highly elated; jubilant; triumphant
FAMINE	= 12.	INMAFE
		Extreme and general scarcity of food, as within a country
IMMERSE	= 13.	RMEEMSI
		To involve deeply; soak; sink totally into
INCESSANTLY	= 14.	INAESLNTYSC
		Continually; without a break
SCIMITARS	= 15.	SRSITCIMA
		Curved Asian swords with the sharp edge on the convex side

VOCABULARY JUGGLE LETTERS 2 *The Alchemist*

_____   = 1. YIIITEVNTUL
                       Through natural insight; without learning

_____   = 2. RNMEITTSTDA
                       Passed; transferred

_____   = 3. YTAECORJTR
                       Path of a projectile or other moving body through space

_____   = 4. TTTRAES
                       Torn or ragged clothing

_____   = 5. NLEETNSSI
                       Guards

_____   = 6. IISSMRATC
                       Curved Asian swords with the sharp edge on the convex side

_____   = 7. SARISYTC
                       A room in a church housing the sacred vessels and vestments

_____   = 8. EAINERFDR
                       Restrained or held back

_____   = 9. RTOANNPTCGISSOIO
                       Forecasts or predictions

_____   = 10. OALSTIANG
                       Sentimental longing for the happiness of a former place or time

_____   = 11. OMNULUIS
                       Brilliant intellectually; enlightening

_____   = 12. NAEERLVT
                       Strong easterly wind in the Mediterranean

_____   = 13. ANENMITLG
                       Expressing sorrow or regret

_____   = 14. EIDVNOK
                       Caused, called forth, or brought about

_____   = 15. HNTZIE
                       A point on the celestial sphere vertically above a given position

VOCABULARY JUGGLE LETTERS 2 ANSWER KEY *The Alchemist*

INTUITIVELY	= 1.	YIIITEVNTUL Through natural insight; without learning
TRANSMITTED	= 2.	RNMEITTSTDA Passed; transferred
TRAJECTORY	= 3.	YTAECORJTR Path of a projectile or other moving body through space
TATTERS	= 4.	TTTRAES Torn or ragged clothing
SENTINELS	= 5.	NLEETNSSI Guards
SCIMITARS	= 6.	IISSMRATC Curved Asian swords with the sharp edge on the convex side
SACRISTY	= 7.	SARISYTC A room in a church housing the sacred vessels and vestments
REFRAINED	= 8.	EAINERFDR Restrained or held back
PROGNOSTICATIONS	= 9.	RTOANNPTCGISSOIO Forecasts or predictions
NOSTALGIA	= 10.	OALSTIANG Sentimental longing for the happiness of a former place or time
LUMINOUS	= 11.	OMNULUIS Brilliant intellectually; enlightening
LEVANTER	= 12.	NAEERLVT Strong easterly wind in the Mediterranean
LAMENTING	= 13.	ANENMITLG Expressing sorrow or regret
INVOKED	= 14.	EIDVNOK Caused, called forth, or brought about
ZENITH	= 15.	HNTZIE A point on the celestial sphere vertically above a given position

www.ingramcontent.com/pod-product-compliance
Lightning Source LLC
Chambersburg PA
CBHW051404070526
44584CB00023B/3289